FLANNERY O'CONNOR AND EDWARD LEWIS WALLANT

Two of a Kind

John V. McDermott

University Press of America,® Inc.
Lanham · Boulder · New York · Toronto · Oxford

Copyright © 2005 by
University Press of America,® Inc.
4501 Forbes Boulevard
Suite 200
Lanham, Maryland 20706
UPA Acquisitions Department (301) 459-3366

PO Box 317
Oxford
OX2 9RU, UK

All rights reserved
Printed in the United States of America
British Library Cataloging in Publication Information Available

Library of Congress Control Number: 2005929537
ISBN 0-7618-3269-6 (paperback : alk. ppr.)

∞™ The paper used in this publication meets the minimum
requirements of American National Standard for Information
Sciences—Permanence of Paper for Printed Library Materials,
ANSI Z39.48—1984

DEDICATION

For Catherine, my beloved wife,

and for our four children,

Kathleen, Laura Anne, John, and Mary

Contents

Acknowledgments		vii
Introduction		ix
Chapter 1	A Shared Vision	1
Chapter 2	Correlative Themes	5
Chapter 3	The Holocaust	17
Chapter 4	Methods of Presentation I Allegory—Parables—Biblical Allusions	29
Chapter 5	Methods of Presentation II Symbols—Using People, Places, and Things	47
Chapter 6	Methods of Presentation III The Grotesque—Exaggeration and Violence	61
Chapter 7	Methods of Presentation IV Imagery: Realistic and Romantic	65
Chapter 8	Humor and Compassion	67
Chapter 9	Humanism: Secular and Christian and the Intertwining Philosophical Attitudes	73
Works Cited		79
Index		85
About the Author		93

Acknowledgments

I am indebted to Reverend Robert Lauder, my mentor, Professor of Philosophy at St. John's University in Jamaica, New York; Dr. James Hafley, Professor of English, who introduced me to the works of Edward Lewis Wallant; and Dr. George Cevasco, Professor of English, who made me aware of the works of Flannery O'Connor.

I would also like to acknowledge my sister Barbara Ann McDermott for her reading and expert editing of the text in its several stages.

In addition, I wish to thank the following publishers for permission to quote from the works indicated. Harold Ober Associates, Inc., for the following works by Edward Lewis Wallant: *The Human Season, The Tenants of Moonbloom,* and *The Children at the Gate;* Harcourt, Inc. for *The Pawnbroker* by Edward Lewis Wallant; and Farrar, Strauss, and Giroux, LLC for the following works by Flannery O'Connor: *The Complete Stories by Flannery O'Connor,* "The Violent Bear It Away" and *Wise Blood.*

Introduction

In style and in substance, the fiction of Flannery O'Connor and Edward Lewis Wallant leads to a convergence seldom seen in literature. Their methods of presentation run parallel on many points, but above and beyond all these parallel points lies a more significant one—a vision of man deeply spiritual in nature. Theirs is a singular, shared vision that focused on man's final destiny. They recognized that man is more than flesh and bone, that he has an elemental urge, a "homing instinct" (Kinney 78) for God that cannot possibly be satisfied by anything this world might offer as substitute. Both writers were preoccupied essentially with the meaning of man's existence—his understanding of himself, his relationship with his fellow man, and his relationship to God. In a word, Ms. O'Connor and Mr. Wallant were spiritual soulmates.

Nicholas Ayo first noted Mr. Wallant's affinity to Ms. O'Connor:

> Although Wallant is often compared to Nathaniel West . . . Flannery O'Connor's grim realism and quiet affirmation also suggest a rich comparison, [for] both novelists explore deeply within the soul of sinful man and repeatedly cry out for a change of heart. (86)

The similar nature of their ingrained spirituality has also been noted by Louis D. Rubin. He points out how "their similar values [are] different from modern times" (281). He notes that O'Connor "brilliantly explores the moral and religious dimensions of Southern experience [with a] burning moral image of human life" (278), and that Wallant, too, employed "the highly developed inward spirituality . . . of the Ghetto and the Synagogue" (279) in his fiction. Both, Rubin finds, faced the challenge of "equating [their] spiritual identity with [a] secular society" (279).

The major focus of this researcher will center on the novels of the two writers rather than their short stories with the only exception occurring when a significant point made in an O'Connor story relates directly to an idea being discussed. The text will reveal chapter by chapter the multiple, parallel ways in which both writers express their desire to study the inner life of man. Wallant himself said, "All my novels are character studies whose purpose is to illuminate the life inside a human being" (Raper 37).

Some of the primary components addressed that will substantiate the unique correlation between the two will include their shared vision, their parallel themes, their similar methods of presentation, their studied use of symbols, their fusion of two realms of literature—the Romantic and the Realistic—their compassion and humor, their perspective on the Holocaust, and their humanism.

What is somewhat surprising is that, despite the numerous points of convergence on their insight into the mystery of man and his existence and in their mutual methods of presentation of these concepts, no evidence exists that these two knew of each other's existence—much less of each other's writings. It is surprising because they lived within the same four decades of the twentieth century. Ms. O'Connor was born in 1925, Mr. Wallant in 1926; she died in 1964, he in 1962. Sarah Gordon, current senior editor of the *Flannery O'Connor Bulletin*, has said that in her 25 years of research and writing about O'Connor, she never heard of any verbal or written communication between the two. But despite this total ignorance of each other, the fact remains that in giving top priority to "understanding the truth about people" (Hicks 136) and in their stress on the need for man to escape the prison of the self, both were united in spiritual accord and in their memorable dramatization of man's purpose in life.

Both writers received early high praise. In 1970, Granville Hicks wrote that "of all the young writers of promise in the postwar period, none seem to be more extraordinary than Flannery O'Connor" (Foreword), whereas Ernest Becker gave equally high praise to Wallant:

> Edward Lewis Wallant [is] another of those young geniuses—like Kafka—whose emotional and intuitive insight into the human condition [is] astonishing. . . . He has proven himself a rare student of the character of man, and assured himself a place among the select few who can penetrate into the heart of the human condition (75).

David D. Galloway also remarks on Wallant's talent: "Edward Lewis Wallant . . . promises to be one of the most significant novelists of his generation" (54), and Alfred Kazin pays additional high tribute to O'Connor: "She is not just the best woman writer of this time and place. . . . She was a genius" (Back cover of *3 by Flannery O'Connor*). Thus, despite the fact that both writers were included in a text entitled *Minor American Novelists*, edited by Charles Ava Hoyt, a reading of O'Connor's and Wallant's fiction will reveal how inappropriate the term "minor" is in relation to the two. Hoyt himself said, "I shall not be surprised if future critics award him [Wallant] a high place in our literature on the basis of the four novels" (118). This assessment has been proven true in Ms. O'Connor's case on the basis of her two novels and thirty-one short stories. Their works define their major contributions to American literature.

Chapter 1

A Shared Vision

Though Flannery O'Connor and Edward Lewis Wallant never met, they echoed each other in their concern for man's ultimate destiny. This concern was dramatized by a religious vision that each possessed. The thematic core of both writers' works centered on man's attempt to get beyond himself, to recognize the existence of another, and in so doing realize a spiritual rebirth, a state of "becoming" (Quinn 529). When this process occurs, the protagonists are awarded a sense of well-being that they had never thought possible, if indeed they had ever contemplated the necessity of such a radical change in themselves. Both Ms. O'Connor and Mr. Wallant point out man's myopic vision, a condition that emanates from his immersion into the self. Just before his death, Wallant wrote: "I suggest that most people are nearsighted, myopic in their ability to perceive the details of human experience" (3418).

Wallant's pervasive religious vision is stated clearly by his friend Seymour Epstein:

> Ed Wallant didn't stop worrying for a minute, worrying about the human race, wanting it better than it was. {His work} involves understanding and forgiveness at a deep and transcending level. Every novel Ed Wallant wrote contained . . . honesty, understanding and forgiveness. (9-10)

David D. Galloway is another who assents to Wallant's focus on man's spiritual life: "Wallant's recurring theme was man's capacity for spiritual regeneration, and he sounded it with increasing joy and authority throughout his brief literary career" (Preface to Edward Lewis Wallant).

Without bypassing this world, both writers were "always aware of the transient quality of life. . . . [Both wrote] of pain and sadness, of agony and God, [of people] disturbed and seeking" (Ribalow 327). Kenneth C. Russell notes that Wallant's *The Human Season* "describes one stage in the process of man's spiritual development. Wallant's hero (Joe Berman) struggles forward and is granted a measure of insight" (62). This novel, Russell thinks, is "an apt illustration of fiction's ability to take hold of reality in such a way that we not only experience the facts which preoccupy theology's intellectual approach, but the resonance of feeling which often evades it" (62).

It may be seen that both Wallant's and O'Connor's characters "look to an essence beyond existence" (Davis 12). For Wallant, this concern for man's "essence beyond existence" is one of primary importance. He asks, "Are we not . . . insane children hastening toward our own extinction because we have struggled to extinguish those vast, elemental urges which argue for perpetuity, which ultimately affirm life?" (Marovitz 176). This "vast, elemental urge" he speaks of is synonymous with O'Connor's belief that "humanity possesses an indelible divine imprint for God that makes the heart restless until it finds its peace in His will" (Kinney 81). O'Connor's and Wallant's personal motives for writing as they do reveal their congruent aims. O'Connor said, "An artist [is] ultimately concerned with . . . spiritual matters as the truths of the human heart" (Wray 88) with which Wallant clearly agrees: "Seeing is the key word, seeing with the heart, with the brain, with they eye. . . . There are times when we have a need we cannot recognize, a rudely awakened hunger to know what lies in the hearts of others" (The Artist's Eyesight 1). And as Walter Shear has noted, for O'Connor too, "Vision is a key metaphor in the interaction and conflict between different modes of expression" (141). And just as Wallant wrote about "How people spoke and acted under . . . stresses" (Epstein 10), so O'Connor's main interest is in what happens to the character . . . when he is suddenly thrown outside his personal and cultural resources into a premonition of the indefinite, which is not only beyond all previous calculations, but beyond all calculations he might [ever] make" (Shear 141).

It is significant that O'Connor, a Catholic, and Wallant, a Jew, refused to limit their fiction by addressing it specifically to Catholic or Jewish readers. Both were concerned with universal humanity; their fellow human being was not simply a Catholic or a Jew. Being all-inclusive, their vision encompassed every individual. As Wallant said, "So I am a Jew—but I am not primarily concerned with Jewry. . . . I try to share the larger human denominator" (E.L. Wallant personal letter). And in O'Connor's case, Gerald R. Russello notes, "We can still speak of a universal Catholic imagination in which American writers [like O'Connor] . . . share a definite world view that separates them from other American writers" (210). Ted R. Spivey also stresses O'Connor's emphasis on the spiritual condition of universal man when he writes, "Even Flannery O'Connor, who considered her Catholicism the most important fact of her existence, told Granville Hicks, 'I'm not interested in sects as sects; I'm concerned with the religious individual'" (90).

In O'Connors novel *Wise Blood*, vision plays a primary role. The protagonist, Hazel Motes, like Wallant's Angelo DeMarco in *The Children at the Gate*, disdains mystery. Hazel "wanted to stay in Eastrod, his two eyes open, his hands handling familiar things, his feet on the known track" (16). But in his later spiritual transformation we read: "The whole black world in his head—his head bigger than the world, his head big enough to include the sky, and planets and whatever was or had been or would be" (19). His is finally a vision that extends beyond space and time, a vision of eternity, one which Mrs. Flood, his landlady, in her myopic vision cannot even begin to glimpse though she tries: "She sat staring with eyes shut" (126) into Motes' singularly focused vision of meaning that lies beyond the worldly appearance of things. O'Connor then stresses Mrs. Flood's earth-bound vision by calling her "Mrs. Flood, the landlady" (118). She is at home in this world, unable to see what Haze, now blind, can clearly see. He has obliterated for himself all things that would block his vision of eternity: "She had to imagine the pinpoint of light. . . . She saw it as some kind of star, like the star on Christmas cards" (119). She, Mrs. Flood, saw him moving farther and farther into the darkness until he was the pinpoint of light" (126) at one with the light of the world, the risen Christ.

Since Wallant and O'Connor were essentially spiritual or religious writers, they knew the individual must see with more than what "William Blake called 'single vision' [that is to] see objectively, [what] only . . . meets the eye. [These are the people who Blake believed] take the world and language at face value" (Kessler 211). Vision, as a metaphor for both writers "is a microcosm: the ever present, ever varying conjunction of the known and the unknown" (211). Speaking about O'Connor's vision, Shannon Burns also notes that the essence of O'Connor is not to limit, but to expand vision. She attempts to show the reader that "'reality' has many dimensions" (113). And in referring to Wallant, Max F. Schulz adds: "Wallant's was a religious temperament which dealt with this secular . . . century . . . with an unremediating imagination that miraculously retained its exhilaration; his was a tragic vision which expresses an unequivocal reverence for life" (39). Both were firm believers in mystery.

Chapter 2

Correlative Themes

Three themes Wallant and O'Connor focused on were man's quest for satisfaction of the soul, the mystery of man's being and reason for his existence, and the necessity of suffering. Martha Dula noted that in terms "of Flannery O'Connor's . . . portrayals of life, [there is a] hunger in man that is the central element of human existence" (11). O'Connor said that the "hunger which grips modern man is a continuous endless process. . . . Man's hunger [she says] is an eternal condition" (10). Ms. Dula thinks that in *Wise Blood*, it is "only in death [that Hazel Motes] finds complete satisfaction for his 'hunger'. And in terms of Miss O'Connor's perspective on a corrupt world, redemption is possible only through an extreme act, an act of absolute irrevocable sacrifice" (7, 10).

In *Wise Blood*, Haze's search for truth is foreshadowed: "His eyes . . . don't look like they see what he's looking at but they keep on looking" (62). At this point, though Haze does not yet realize it, he is seeking something beyond the appearance of things. His earlier protestation, "I am clean" (53) is somewhat tempered by his further remark, "If Jesus existed, I wouldn't be clean" (53). He knows what Christ proclaimed but is adamant in his rejection of Him. We read: "An owl [a creature synonymous with wisdom] shuts its eyes softly [and turns] its face to the wall" (55) when Motes protests his innocence. In his later blind, all-seeing state, he confesses, "I'm not clean" (122). Ms. O'Connor has Mrs. Flood voice the changes in Motes: '"He might as well be in a Monkery.'" [Mrs. Flood] "saw him going back to Bethlehem and she had to laugh" (119). But, as it turns out, she speaks only the truth. As he moves toward Christ in death, we read that his "fragile broken face [has become] tranquil [and] more composed than Mrs. Flood had ever observed" (126). The landlady, Dula thinks, stands as a portrayal of the nature of the individual's eternal longing, for so long as evil exists in the world, there will be millions of . . . human beings still searching . . . and some like Hazel Motes will find absolution" (Dula 11).

In Edward Lewis Wallant's *The Tenants of Moonbloom*, the protagonist Norman Moonbloom also hungers for some unrealized "something" (117). In his quest to emerge from the "hermetic globe" (24) he has immersed himself in, he is able to do so only by recognizing there are other people in this world who are like himself, worthy of compassion and love. In Wallant's fiction, it is this loving compassion for another that will satisfy one's hunger. It is the only way by which the human being can fully realize himself, to become "fully alive" (31) to the existence of others. In the novel, Basellecci expresses this viewpoint in sincere and succinct terms: "I become carried off. One forgets that things exist outside yourself. You live alone and you become susceptible to obsessions. I admit, things get out of proportion, magnified. There is a selfishness involved thinking only of yourself" (81).

In two of his other novels, *The Children at the Gate* and *The Pawnbroker*, we witness Wallant's adherence to O'Connor's belief in "absolute sacrifice," the "extreme act" of redemption, on the part of Sammy in *The Children at the Gate* and on the part of Jesus Ortiz in *The Pawnbroker*. In their sacrificial acts, they help Angelo DeMarco and Sol Nazerman see the significance of communing with others. Their acts communicate Wallant's vision that all men are of value and in need of one another's forgiveness and love.

Jonathan Baumbach and Iris Conchita Rabasca are in agreement when they speak of the quest theme in each writer's work. Baumbach thinks that "if one had to abstract from [Wallant's] novels a unifying concern, a characteristic of seriousness, it would be [man's] spiritual passage from guilt to redemption" (Baumbach 15), whereas Rabasca notes that O'Connor, like Wallant, makes "a distinction between finite and transcendent reality and assumes the presence of a supernatural world within the natural" (3963A). Both writers, according to Rabasca, "structured [their fiction] around the archetypes of spiritual exile, epiphany, and journey home [and] in both literatures the journey out of exile is often precipitated by violence. [And both, adds Rabasca] hold up to the light the moral failings of their societies and point the way to redemption" (3963A).

Equally striking and significant to the quest theme in the fiction of both writers is the mystery of man's being. For O'Connor, "Mystery is the essential man, the whole man becoming, developing his human potential and promise, struggling to complete his integrity through love. In O'Connor's mind, love is never an accomplished fact but always a continuing struggle. And man is never a problem to be solved but a mystery to be respected" (Quinn 520).

Edward Lewis Wallant echoes O'Connor's beliefs on the inexplicable essence of man, the mystery that is man. He stresses his own "need [to] recognize . . . what lies in the hearts of others" (The Artist's Eyesight 1). In *The Children at the Gate*, Louis D. Rubin notes that Sammy "forces Angelo, the man of reason, to realize that not only is there an essential mystery to human life that cannot be explained through systems, but neither may the mystery be ignored or glossed over" (271). John G. Parks also notes that in this same novel, "The absurd man, the man of passion, Sammy, has overcome the rational man of logic (Angelo)" (116). Wallant accents in this novel the complex mystery that is man, much as Dostoyevski did in his fiction. Parks points out that Dostoyevski believed that "The whole work of man seems to consist of nothing but proving to himself every minute that he is a man and not a piano key" (Parks 116). Again, Parks notes in Wallant's *The Tenants of Moonbloom* that Norman Moonbloom is "one [in whom] one of the major questions the novel is asking . . . what is man, if his chief good and market of his time be but sleep and feed? A beast no more" (116). Wallant, it is evident, is like O'Connor in his desire to center on the mystery of man's nature. Ernest Becker is another who points out Wallant's preoccupation with mystery. He calls "*The Pawnbroker* a true work of art because it points beyond what it reveals. [It makes us] ponder . . . the wider questions of man's fate" (Becker 98). And referring to this same novel, Stephen Karpowitz comments that the question of Sol Nazerman's mystery, the history of the conscience it reveals, and the twin feelings (love and revenge) it stirs to life in Ortiz are of major concerns to the novel" (52).

In *The Human Season*, Joe Berman, the protagonist, finally accepts the inscrutable presence of God in the world, which allows him to attain faith. But his concession to mystery, which he articulates in the phrase "Ah, well" (160), is voiced, although "empathically" (160), with a tone of resignation. His faith is like a "light that doesn't last long, but once you've seen it is enough" (160. Berman voices this faith, this "last hope . . . almost desperately" (160) as if he is trying to convince himself of its validity. However strong it is or is not, it is better than the anguished state of despair he had gone through before reaching this spiritual awakening. Earlier, before his soul-searching change, he has disdained mystery. Each problem that arose in his work as a plumber had its solution. His work "held no mysteries for him" (19). But his wife Mary's death punctured his sense of invulnerability, as did his son's. Berman "wallowed in puzzlement [and] kept himself submerged in a counterfeit surprise even after he had sensed the first touch of alarm" (42). For Berman, mystery generated fear. "Something threatened . . . sleep itself. It was coffin-like, black and heedless as space. From within its dark confines he railed against it, scratched desperately at it as though with his fingernails on its massive lid. He strained for human consciousness. To Know, to know and finally he raised the cover of massive slumber. . . . Something abominable was in the room with him; someone or something. . . . His flesh tingled with the thrill of fear" (23).

When Berman later begins to analyze his behavior, he is forced to confront mystery, something he had avoided and denigrated all his life because he had lived his life with reason at its foundation. He believed in *knowing*, not in *feeling*, its alternative. He began to suffer "at the great mystery put upon him [to] . . . Hear things that were out of hearing , see things that were transparent, while only a few feet away . . . and he would be in both places" (138). Early in his life he had what may be termed a mystical experience. This experience occurred when he was with his father at the river. When he gains a "first sight of the river . . . it appeared a broad, living reflection of the lightening sky . . . its sound up close was soft, yet all-embracing that it gave an impression of great volume . . . and Berman sensed . . . the real power and movement were underneath that flat, reflecting surface, beyond his ability to measure or even guess at" (136). Then we see the river as the voice of God calling to him:

> He knew the rushing voice of the river, suddenly very close as though it had held a silence at their approach, waiting to thunder at them so they would give it attention [and then] a boat appeared on the broad current. A peasant and a boy were bent over the net . . . suddenly they pulled the net up into the boat, tumbling a confusion of silver. The man looked toward the wagon rumbling along the deserted dawn road. He called out something in a hoarse voice. Then he held the fish aloft in his hand, a shape of brief sparkle and brilliance. Berman gasped as though transfixed by something beyond naming. His little sound brought

his father's head around. . . . Berman pointed as though in apology toward the man holding the fish aloft on the river. His father followed his gesture, studied the simple sight with an expression of perplexity. . . . Finally he turned back to his son. They held their eyes locked for just a few seconds, both puzzled now . . . until finally the father nodded slowly at the boy, confirming something wondrous to him, something he could have all the time in the world to find out (136-137).

It takes nearly 50 years for Berman "to find out [what] the something wondrous" (137) was. Back in the present as "he sat before the television his attention was broken up by a . . . nervousness, as though something waited just beyond his ken, something to be recognized" (140). He sits "old and lonely . . . waiting for some sort of . . . what?—to be announced" (141). And then back into the past he goes and "stands in the river wind and watches the Christian peasants netting their fishes . . . feels the hidden urging of the cold river" (141). This sight causes him to break into an "open smile" (140-141). In his return to the past, he continually hears the river singing, but this preoccupation with the sound of the river gnaws at Berman's mind. Still in darkness he asks, "What is it all about?" [and, as Wallant writes,] "he was not through with it, that he had at least a little of the answer to find" (144).

As the novel ends, Berman comes to recognize the voice of God, that "towering presence" (76) as the voice of the river that has been reaching out to him. When he comes to faith, "He had no words . . . for the thing he was sure of" (159). Berman's journey to faith has been a painful one. Despite any lingering doubts, he has come to believe. His "Ah, well" (160) suggests his assent to mystery, or to phrase it another way, he realizes man's reasoning may at times be quite unreasonable.

In *The pawnbroker*, Sol Nazerman comes to terms with his life by way of mystery through intuition and through feeling. Knowing finally it is impossible to bury the past, he comes to see that all men are not evil. In seeing this truth, he is able to forgive himself and his fellow brethren. On the novel's final page we read: The pawnbroker was counting his losses and forgiving himself as he watched the river" (279). In forgiving himself, he is able to sympathize with his fellow human beings. Early in the novel he is bent on isolating himself from others. But there are moments, when "for some unknown reason" (48), he exhibits minute, innate signs of goodness. His effect on his assistant Jesus Ortiz as the novel concludes is a salutary one for both. Ortiz was intrigued by the "pawnbroker's mysterious history" (71). He sought to discover the mystery of Nazerman's being. We read, "He [Jesus Ortiz] crouched in the imminence of revelation, oddly eased and enriched in the things beyond what he could form in thought, beyond what the other man said" (75). In answer to his belief that "nothing in the world makes sense" (29), Ortiz finds an answer in the mystery attached to the pawnbroker's spirit. This world of sense provides him no answers; his sacrificial act in which he saves Nazerman's life but loses his own is generated by a spirit of love that had lain dormant in his soul, but which was activated by his belief in the pawnbroker's true inner goodness. His belief in Nazerman's inner goodness is ignited through a mystical intuition, a gratuitous act of grace, that inspires him and gives him the courage to deny himself for the welfare of another. In moving toward the answer to the mystery of Nazerman's elusive spirit, "Ortiz imagined himself approaching a great light in the earth, filled with immense trembling excitement, not knowing the source of the light, moving toward it and wondering whether it would be fearsome or exalting" (71). Like Joe Berman in *The Human Season*, Ortiz moves toward a "light" (70), but not one "that doesn't last long" (160), but rather one that he will follow into eternity. His sacrificial act assures him of this future.

In Wallant's last novel, *The Tenants of Moonbloom*, mystery again plays a conspicuous role. Norman Moonbloom, the protagonist, begins to feel a mysterious change in himself: "Something profound had changed in him and he sought to recognize it" (117). He begins to contemplate mystery: "Most of my life I thought that mystery was only in things that had nothing to do with me" (131). As his character finally transcends itself beyond its mortal trappings, he comes to the full knowledge of the cause of his transformation. "For the first time, people entered me . . . and I didn't know how to get them out" (150). With this admission, Norman's life has reached the beginnings of its fulfillment. His change, like Joe Berman's and Sol Nazerman's, from isolated man to a more complete human being has its first fissure when Norman begins to ponder the mystery of his being: "He didn't know why he was the way he was. [He deprecates himself.] I'm a small man of definite limitations" (23). This self-assessment proves to be the novel's most ironic statement, considering his amazing change of character.

It is his relations with his tenants, whom he initially abhorred, that he begins to feel a change in himself: "'Something is happening to me,' he thought. He had never felt quite like this" (152). Though several of the tenants begin to see his metamorphosis, it is Paxton who sees his transition from a man immersed in himself to one of complete selflessness: "You're changing, Dad, what is it with you?" (137). Paxton sees Moonbloom as a man apart, a man invested in the realm of mystery. "You are an extraordinary case—not typical of homo-sapiens" (45). The antagonism that earlier had interpenetrated Moonbloom's relations with the tenants fades unalterably into a relationship beneficent to both. At the novel's conclusion "a great serenity seemed to wrap around them all. . . . He was united with all of them." (159-160).

Ironically, the reason for Moonbloom's mysterious transformation is initiated by his attempt to deny any possibility of change; on the contrary, he made every effort to escape from its "claws" (8). "There were things that Norman Moonbloom did not want to know" (21). For him, the meaning of man's existence was irrelevant; he felt life "doesn't mean anything. . . . It [simply] is" (31). In his gradual metamorphosis, he begins to realize "that he had no way of avoiding whatever it was that had happened to him" (57). Norman begins to understand that "whatever it was" (57) is his becoming "fully alive" (31), something which heretofore he had "never considered" (31).

In Moonbloom's transformation, we read of its mysterious identity; it was a "mysterious mysticism to which he was now subject" (138). What he does not yet comprehend is that this mysticism is invoked by the tenants' agonies, those human agonies that cry out for easement are the mystical gifts being presented to him by God. "He sat in his formerly peaceful room and wondered anew at the presentations he was being offered with increasing intensity" (119). Realizing "something profound had changed in him . . . he sought to recognize" (117) it. He is naturally apprehensive about the effects of his transformation. Wallant's precise imagery insinuates Moonbloom's perplexity, "He stopped next to a street lamp and put his hand on his head. 'I don't know, I don't know,'" he said in a shocked voice to the evening" (80).

As the novel concludes, Norman, as a man transformed is filled with joyful gratitude because of his acceptance of and his acceptance by the tenants. He is stunned by what has been given him: "I never dreamed there was this. It will kill me" (127). And it truly does kill his old ego-centered self. His non-belief has been transformed. "'Oh, God,' he said in an ashy light, 'all this for me?'" (123). He felt "as if he were walking . . . on great wooden sticks that made him feel so tall" (142). He "howls with unthinkable ecstasy . . . . 'I'm born'" (158), and so he is.

In his third, but last published novel, *The Children at the Gate*, Wallant focuses on the theme once again of mystery versus reason. Sammy Abel Kahan, the novel's protagonist, may be seen as the incarnate symbol of mystery. As mystery incarnate, he affects all the other characters, especially Angelo DeMarco, the confirmed man of reason. It is the mystery of Sammy's being in its invisible but active essence that antagonizes Angelo. This presence of mystery as an unseen yet viable entity affects Angelo despite his efforts to deny or diminish it. In his frustration, he disdains Sammy's bizarre actions. He is overwhelmed by the enigma of Sammy's personality. But in his arrogant pride, he proclaims, "You're no mystery to me" (82). It is indeed the mystery of Sammy's being that provokes Angelo into admitting: "I don't know what you are to me. That's what bothers me because . . . the truth is you been bugging me plenty" (121). Still, despite Sammy's mysterious influence on him, Angelo continues to reject him. "All your spooky talk isn't any mysterious cloud, it's a lot of dust" (130).

In his attempt to attribute man's actions to strictly biological sources, Angelo tries to avert the idea of one segment of mystery—man's conscience. Yet despite his cynicism and his avoidance of contemplating the invisible workings of conscience, he reprimands his cousin Frank for his habitual cheating of his customers. "Don't your conscience ever bother you?" (13).

Sammy's talk continuously mystifies Angelo—"You won't ever listen to things that don't make a sound" (128)—for Angelo is only caught up in sensible things. In his outrageous parables, Sammy speaks of the mystery of love. It emanates from the most unlikely characters in his stories, but characters alike in their listening to the silent vibrations of their hearts. It is telling to note that Angelo is finally changed spiritually, not through or by any formalistic rituals or any intellectual accommodations to faith, but by the ministry of love and compassion that identifies Sammy and is his mission in life.

Just as the "light" ignites faith in Joe Berman's heart in *The Human Season* and Jesus Ortiz's in *The Pawnbroker*, so in *The Children at the Gate*, "light" stands as a symbol of movement toward understanding that mystery is real and a motivation to faith. Sammy asks Angelo, "Do you know where you're going? . . . "Come on, I got a flashlight. I'll light you" (29). And so he does. Sammy's light becomes a stepping stone to lead Angelo out of his spiritual darkness. Ironically, Angelo makes an entreaty for the light though he does not realize its full power. "Look, if you're gonna hold that light for me. . . ." (31).

In the novel, it is Angelo's continual dependence on the visible that has prevented him from seeing the truth incarnate in Sammy's being. Sammy's injunction to him to "close [his] eyes and listen to the nothing (161) is finally acceded to by Angelo. "He never wanted again to miss hearing what happened in silence" (183). His transformation from a man of the senses to a man of the spirit appears complete.

In Flannery O'Connor's *The Violent Bear It Away*, the child, Bishop, is one who is the essence of mystery. He represents spiritual perfection. He affects everyone he meets, and his presence evokes either awe or anger. No one can remain indifferent to him. He deeply disturbs his own mother: "She could not express her exact revulsion, for her feeling was not logical. . . . Bishop's face was like the look of a face she had seen in some medieval painting where the martyr's limbs are being sawed off, and his expression says he is not being deprived of nothing essential" (230). In her absence of faith, she sees his face as expressing perversity. For her, the "obvious good" (230) refers only to physical, worldly goods. Since Bishop is the epitome of spiritual goodness, his being is foreign to her.

Another minor character who is struck by Bishop's presence is the waitress at the Cherokee Lodge. She treats him kindly, bewitched by his face—"She gazed fascinated into his mysterious face" (223)—but for Tarwater, the novel's protagonist who lives in spiritual darkness, Bishop's presence "was a black spot in the glare of his vision" (222). At this point in the novel, Tarwater's insight into Bishop as savior is completely hidden from him because he wants it that way. He had professed no need for Christ; he would be his own savior.

Rayber, the man of reason, also rejects Bishop, even though "moments would . . . come rushing from some inexplicable part of himself [when] he would experience a love for the child so outrageous he would be shocked" (92). By not truly believing in the mystery of Bishop's existence, Bishop's meaning eludes him. That, like Lucifer, he had a knowledge of God's existence, is evident. Rayber "did not believe that he himself was formed in the image and likeness of God but that Bishop was he had no doubt" (192). In his enormous pride, he knows there is a God, but it is a God he refuses to serve.

After Bishop drowns, Rayber collapses; he "stood waiting for the intolerable hurt that was his due . . . until he realized there would be no pain [then] he collapsed" (243). Rayber, to his deep regret, realizes he has lost the capacity to feel. He realizes he cannot suffer as man does. He collapses because he has lost his humanity, and with it, his soul. This dire ending of Rayber is foreshadowed earlier, for when "Bishop gazed at him . . . a dreadful sense of loss came over him" (233). Rayber desired his own end, for he believed that "to feel nothing was peace" (241). He realized too late how wrong he was. In feeling "nothing" (241) he had extinguished the last spark of goodness within himself.

For Edward Lewis Wallant, a change in character is driven by a mysterious impulse, something within the character that he cannot name. For Flannery O'Connor, this mysterious impulse may be defined as *grace*, God's extending His hand to man to help him find his way. Men, like Hazel Motes in *Wise Blood*, are given the chance to see themselves in the light of truth. In Motes' case, when he sees how blind he has been in recognizing his true inner self, he literally blinds himself to all worldly illusions. His landlady, Mrs. Flood, due to her worldly immersion, cannot penetrate Motes' cauterizing vision that has burned away all impediments to truth of self. For those like Mrs. Flood, who "like the clear light of day . . . [who] liked to see things, worldly realities" (113), there is small hope of her envisioning her true self. She is like Julian Chestny in O'Connor's "Everything That Rises Must Converge," who, like Wallant's Norman Moonbloom before his change, had lived immersed in a "mental bubble" (11) which had thwarted his any attempt to see the reality of himself. Julian's earlier taunt to his mother, "You aren't who you think you are" (22) proves to be an ironic boomerang when his words are applied to himself. He is at the story's end a man without a "voice" (23) or "identity" (21). He has been granted his wish to feel "free of the general idiocy of his fellows" (11), and to his rue, his hate-filled act of rejecting his mother—"He had ceased to recognize her existence" (14)—retaliates against him: "Trying to determine his identity . . . she found nothing familiar abut him" (21).

In Wallant's *The Tenants of Moonbloom*, Norman is saved when he allows people to "enter him" (150). In O'Connor's "Everything That Rises Must Converge," Julian Chestny is not saved because he shields himself from others. And in shattering his self-illusions, Hazel Motes avoids Julian's dire fate. In Wallant, man, driven by a mysterious "something," comes "fully alive" (*Tenants of Moonbloom* 31) to the existence of others and in so doing begets and receives love. In O'Connor, the mysterious "something" called *grace* affects people in different ways.

She knows some will accept it and be changed by it whereas others will not. Wallant's chief characters—Joe Berman, Sol Nazerman, Angelo DeMarco, and Norman Moonbloom—along with O'Connor's Hazel Motes and Marion Francis Tarwater suffer the pain and joy of self-enlightenment.

On the problem of the mystery of suffering, Wallant and O'Connor are of one and the same mind. Richard Fein points out that "an important theme in all of Wallant's novels [is that] all his characters [have to] confront the suffering of other people during [their] own crisis of confusion and introspection. . . . Sol Nazerman tries to deal with all of the people who enter his pawnshop daily and ask something of him, more than he can give, [but he] is a man of no allegiance; the Nazi experience has burned them all away" (71-72). Fein also adds that "it is Wallant . . . who exposed the problem of the Jew who sees the world only in terms of his awareness of his or his people's sufferings in this century" (75).

For Wallant, Max Schulz says that "suffering still has its traditional meaning [that] all good comes only through suffering. [Wallant] confronts each of his alienated . . . heroes with this harsh truth" (37-38). Schulz also says that "acceptance of his existence is a painful process for each of Wallant's protagonists, but if we would be human and whole, we have no alternative to . . . redemptive anguish [for] the exhilaration that overcomes one, and which is a communicable gift to others, more than compensates for the pain" (35).

In O'Connor's writing, "the endings of her stories . . . hint at the possibility of redemption for those who accept their initiation into suffering" (Oliver 5). "In . . . O'Connor, physical imperfection is a sign of grace. This idea of grace through imperfection . . . is an outgrowth of [her] belief that the true communion of saints is not a communion of love but a communion of suffering [and her] references to box cars and gas ovens . . . [have] . . . the implications of universal suffering" (Curley 159). It is through suffering that Hazel Motes and Marion Francis Tarwater come to self-enlightenment, and this self-awakening is also true of Wallant's major protagonists.

Chapter 3

The Holocaust

The theme of suffering is nowhere more dramatically evoked than in the modern day catastrophic horror of the Holocaust. Wallant's *The Pawnbroker* reveals most graphically the obscene tortures of the mind and the body that the Jewish people suffered. Through not nearly as sharply detailed, Flannery O'Connor's references to the Holocaust reveal her righteous anger toward the event. For O'Connor, it stands as a judgment against mankind, a most shameful event we should never attempt to camouflage or deny. She attacks with subtle, acid vehemence those who dismiss its significance. For O'Connor, this event, which exposed the depths to which humanity may sink, represented evil incarnate. The Holocaust is another example of the singular, philosophical view of both writers on the nature of man in all its complexity—in this case man at his worst.

Alan L. Berger says the criterion for "an authentic response to the Holocaust [lies in its] testing and questioning of human . . . action" (11). If this judgment is true, then both Wallant and O'Connor have met the challenge.

In Wallant, through the protagonist Sol Nazerman's dreams and his reaction to those dreams, which pervade and reverberate throughout *The Pawnbroker*, we certainly witness "the testing and questioning of human . . . action" (11) toward the event, for it is in and through Sol's relations with the other characters that Wallant illustrates man's tortured response to this despicable horror. In Sol's case, the brutal memories are at first intolerable. He cannot bear to recall the atrocities committed against his wife and children, and against others. In his remembrance of its horrors, he has renounced humankind until he is literally stunned into believing that there is still some good in man by his assistant Jesus Ortiz's final act of self-sacrifice. In Wallant, a survivor of the Holocaust comes to see the possibility of redemption through extreme pain and suffering and the finality of death.

In Flannery O'Connor's fiction, man's reaction to the Holocaust is one of chilling, cold indifference. The horrors of the event mean little to her protagonists, and because of this insensitivity, she subjects them in the end to the chastisement and pain that is their due. Her attitude is one of righteous judgment; people, she lets it be known, must come to realize the gravity of disassociating themselves from those who have suffered the trauma of this horrific event. In Wallant's writings, we have an inside, personal reaction to the Holocaust; we participate vicariously in Sol Nazerman's anguish, whereas in O'Connor the perspective is from an outsider's view. The Holocaust, to her characters, was something foreign, something that had little or no bearing on their lives. But for O'Connor herself, the event was an indelible stain on the soul of mankind.

In his review of *The Pawnbroker*, Alan L. Berger says that "Wallant seems to be aware of the ineffable difference between the death camps and other types of suffering" (170), [but he still thinks that] Wallant . . . has simultaneously trivialized and wrongly universalized the Holocaust, while paying scarce attention to historic detail" (165). He says, "it is Wallant's belief that the Holocaustal suffering is but one interchangeable component in the vast machinery of human misery" (167), and in this reasoning he is correct. But are we then to conclude that Nazerman's dream's have no basis in historical fact? Are they then simply fabricated nightmares? The question then arises: Does not the entire novel, in its structure and in its content, reverberate around Nazerman's insufferable memories? The effects of the horror on Nazerman's memories, made vivid and painful by Wallant's artistry, reveal his compassion for the tortured soul. Berger is correct, however, as we have said, that the novel shows Wallant's belief that the pain of the Holocaust survivor "is but one tragedy in a universe where tragedy befalls every man."

Berger and Raymond A. Schroth, S.J., have convincingly pointed out that Sol Nazerman truly represents Everyman in his suffering. Berger writes, "Nazerman becomes fully human . . . only by becoming a kind of Jewish-Christian Everyman" (166) to which Schroth agrees, saying, "Sol's recognition of sin as an historic and communal as well as a personal tragedy urges him to escape it. The novel . . . casts the Jew in the role of universal man. [Nazerman comes to see] pain in the context of expiation" (166). Schroth astutely adds, "Wallant demands much of a public not used to linking love to torture, disintegration and death in so unromantic a way" (98). And this assumption is certainly true. And in its truth, this finding stands as another certified link between Wallant and O'Connor, for in O'Connor's mind "the communion of saints was bound together by suffering" (Curley 159), a suffering that would unite them in love with the Savior who sacrificed His life in His love for them.

O'Connor's treatment of the Holocaust is penetrating in a more general way than Wallant's. There is much less vivid detail in communicating its horrors. In her stories, Ruby Turpin, Mrs. Cope, and Mr. and Mrs. Shortly are outsiders who have heard and seen film clips about the Holocaust, but they have not allowed what they have seen and heard to fully penetrate their minds and hearts. Her characters, in their extreme concern for the self, are blind and deaf to the plight of others. The Holocaust, they think, has no personal connection to their lives; for them it was a foreign problem.

John F. Desmond has noted that "O'Connor sees the Holocaust as a horrifying example of modern sentimentality, which she sees in turn as rooted in an ethic of tenderness that is divorced from the meaning of Christian redemption. [She believed] '. . . popular pity, we mark our gain in sensibility and our loss in vision'" (35). O'Connor thought the "myth of Aryan superiority is a perverse variant of the original myth of the perfectibility of man [which in a case] such as a Down's syndrome child or a hopelessly senile geriatric [who] cannot or does not conform to the theory [tears away the] thin mask of sentimentality . . . to reveal contempt, a contempt which often issues in coercion, terror and death [and which leads to] the gas chambers and forced labor camps [which become the] prime examples of this theory" (36). This ethic, she thought, "denies on [its] theoretical grounds the intrinsic worth of the individual person" (36).

In O'Connor's short story "A Circle in the Fire," the protagonist, Mrs. Cope, receives her comeuppance. She is a pride-filled person who attributes her "good fortune" (*Complete Stories* 190) to herself. She is a self-concerned braggart who feels she is self-sufficient, someone in total control of her life. Her words that proffer thanksgiving to God ring hollow when we consider her extremely self-reliant attitude. When she thanks God for her situation and station in life, she elevates herself above those less fortunate: "Negroes, people in iron lungs, people who live in apartments and Europeans who they put in box cars like cattle and ship to Siberia" (178). In this story the victims of the Holocaust, in being equated with cattle by a pride-filled egotist, may be seen as victims of the myth that leads to a categorizing of people and therefore strips them of their personal "intrinsic worth" (Desmond 36) as individuals of value. Mrs. Cope in this respect may be seen as a dramatic example of Aryan superiority in the flesh. The difference between the Nazi mind-set and hers is that they clearly understand and act to propagate the myth; in Mrs. Cope's case, she does not recognize the evil within herself because her pride blinds her to the fact that in demeaning others, she reveals the warped condition of her own soul. Her pride is like a mask that prevents her from seeing the truth of herself.

In "Revelation," another of O'Connor's best stories, we read of Ruby Turpin, another arrogant egotist, who categorizes people according to their social status. She is another whose soul is warped by this world's values. In her clouded, worldly view "all the classes of people wound up crammed in together in a box car being ridden off to be put into a gas oven" (*Complete Stories* 492). Again, as in "A circle in the Fire," we witness the "demonic view" (Desmond 41) of Mrs. Turpin, who considers herself above those less fortunate. These lesser people are seen as fodder for the elite who do with them as they please—feed them to the dogs or pulverize them into corpses in concentration camps as dramatized by Wallant in *The Pawnbroker*. This Aryan mentality was abhorrent to Ms. O'Connor. Her indictment against this most horrendous happening is made abundantly clear in "Revelation" and in "A Circle in the Fire," but it is in "The Displaced Person" that she portrays her most pointed and vehement denunciation of the Holocaust. In this story Mrs. Shortly, like Mrs. Cope and Ruby Turpin, is most concerned with her own well-being. She thinks the Holocaust has little to do with her life. We read: "Mrs. Shortley recalled a newsreel she had seen once of a small room piled high with bodies of dead naked people all in a heap, their arms and legs tangled together, a head thrust in here, a head there, a foot, a knee, a part that should have been covered up sticking out. . . . Before you realize that it was real . . . the picture changed and a hollow-sounding voice was saying "Time Marches On'" (*Complete Stories* 196). And instead of being touched in any compassionate way by the newsreel, her reaction is one of self-righteousness, "This was the kind of thing that was happening every day in Europe where they had not advanced as in this country" (196). A little later we read: "Again she saw the room piled high with bodies" (198) and again she blinds herself to its profound significance, preoccupying herself with thoughts only of her own survival.

In "The Displaced Person," Mr. Shortley is also concerned solely with his own survival. He ignores completely his wife's passing reference to the unjustifiable deaths of millions of innocent people. In referring to Mr. Guizac, the displaced person and his family, whom she detests, Mrs. Shortley says to her husband, "They're Poles . . . from Poland where all them bodies were stacked up at. You remember all them bodies?" (101). In his rejoinder, in referring to the Guizacs, he reveals his self-consumed tunnel vision: "I give them three weeks here" (201). He cares only that their departure will enable him to keep his job. His indifference to the Holocaust victims reveals the deplorable state of his soul. And in the story, Mrs. Shortley's attitude is just as cold and callous as her husband's. She says, "There was no reason they [the Guizacs] couldn't stay over there and take the places of some of the people who had been killed in their . . . butcherings" (205). In her mind, displaced persons were like replacement parts, replacing those equally insignificant in her worldly scheme of things. Ms. O'Connor's characters in these stories are not unlike the many today who do not wish to consider at all the unholy ramifications of the Holocaust.

When Seymour Epstein says that "Ed Wallant knew that much of life is made up of unpleasant things . . . [and that this realization] involves understanding and forgiveness at a deep and transcending level" (9-10), it is evident that Wallant's belief in redemption through suffering has much to do with his view of the Holocaust. His belief in redemption through suffering is in consonance with O'Connor's thoughts on the spiritual value of suffering.

David D. Galloway is one who disagrees with Alan Berger's feeling that Wallant has "trivialized" the Holocaust. In his text *Edward Lewis Wallant*, Galloway says that "Edward Lewis Wallant's *The Pawnbroker* . . . offers a shockingly graphic portrayal of the horrors of war. Nazerman . . . becomes a pawn, a link in the chain of human exploitation and corruption of which the fragmented, dream-ridden world of the pawnshop is a microcosm [and] . . . [although] only seven scenes in the novel deal with the Nazi death camps, . . . their grim legacy permeates the structure of the novel. . . . [It is] Wallant's genius [that gives particular] distilled examples of the human legacy and oppression" (72).

Bonnie Lyons is another who disagrees with Berger's view. She calls *The Pawnbroker* a "positive American Jewish novel" (114). She thinks that "Nazerman's . . . dream memories are among the most powerful, disturbing images in Holocaust literature" (115), [and she finds the novel has a] "basically positive ending. [Lyons also thinks] Jesus Ortiz's . . . willing sacrifice is efficacious [and that] it awakens Sol from years of psychic numbness and willed blindness. . . . He [Lyons continues] recognizes his love for his pitiful customers and is finally able to cry" (117). She also thinks that "the Holocaust has not broken the terms of the contract between God and man, [for] the religious meaning that ends [the novel] is its deeper response to see the Holocaust itself" (118). In *The Pawnbroker*, Lyons believes that "Wallant intends for his readers to see both profound suffering [but also] the equally profound possibility" (121) of redemption. In Wallant, as well as in O'Connor, this point is made again and again.

Lillian S. Kremer agrees with Berger. She is unhappy with *The Pawnbroker*, and she thinks Ortiz's act is an "instinctive" rather than a willing one, as Lyons maintains. Kremer says that Ortiz's act is prompted by "accidental altruism" (173). This view does not seem entirely valid to me because early in the novel we read of Ortiz's attitude toward the pawnbroker. "He was involved in an odd current of emotions, softened and burned and bound" (75). Even at this early stage, Ortiz's feelings for Nazerman are of a mixed alloy, including that of a "softened" heart as he tries to fathom the mystery of the pawnbroker's being. We also have Nazerman's view of Ortiz's character: "Sol has the vague feeling that there were certain horrors this boy would not commit. In Sol Nazerman's eyes, this was a great deal; there were very few people to whom he attributed even the limitation of evil" (11). It should also be remembered that Ortiz had warned his partners not to shoot Nazerman. "I told them no shooting" (270). As Ortiz lay dying, we read: "There was a strange struggle between them, a silent tugging that left them both bewildered and dazed looking. . . . And the pawnbroker stared just as yearning as a freezing man stares at the last ember of a fire and suddenly sees how lovely the color of light can be. 'What do you want from me, Ortiz?'. . . . [Then as Ortiz dies, his] lips shaped some silent words at him, a curse or a blessing or something else completely? (271). It seems credible to interpret this scene as the epiphany of a mystical union of love, heretofore unexpressed. In view of this finding, I see Ms. Kremer's conclusion about Ortiz's final act to be unfounded. Nazerman, I believe, had thought within himself how "lovely" his relationship to Ortiz truly was. It awakened in him the knowledge that all men are not worthy of mistrust, not all men have within their being a Nazi-like spirit where the good appears vanquished completely.

Ms. Kremer also argues that Ortiz's sacrificial act was not the cause of Sol's regeneration.

> This assessment places excessive emphasis on the importance of one scene at the expense of the rest of the novel, reading it as the source [rather than] an extension of Nazerman's regenerative commitments, including financial support of two families, moral support for an exploited prostitute and dissolution, at grave personal risk, of his business partnership. These acts [Kremer believes] exemplify a pattern of spiritual rebirth in the Jewish manner of repentance and willing commitment to society manifested in charitable behavior toward others. (72-73)

Although some of this argument may be valid, it does not negate the fact that Nazerman's deep-seated anger toward mankind in general had not lessened in any significant degree. He said, "I do not trust God or politics or newspapers or music or art. I do not trust smiles or clothes or buildings or scenery or smells. . . . But most of all, I do not trust people and their talk, for they have created hell with that talk, for they have proved they do not deserve to exist, for what they are" (*The Pawnbroker* 115). And in the particular case of Mabel Wheatly, the "exploited prostitute" (Kremer 72). Nazerman's "moral support" seems totally lacking, when we read: "Take your pitiful flesh away from me . . . just take the money. . . . Get out of here. You sicken me" (*The Pawnbroker* 137). And in reference to the "dissolution . . . of his partnership" (Kremer 73), the cause of this break-up is generated by a guilty conscience; his "manner of repentance" (Kremer 73), though, is a self-indulgent act. The motive for his act is to absolve himself from the stain of hypocrisy. He had condemned Goberman, who was profiting by taking money from his own people, under the pretense of supporting his fellow Jews in Israel. Nazerman now realizes his business connection to Murillo, who profits from prostitution, is just as abominable a facade. It is the thought of being considered a hypocrite that compels him to break up with Murillo. His act of repentance is, therefore, tainted because it is primarily generated by thoughts of self to help him maintain some semblance of self-esteem. And last, though he gives financial support to two families, this action is not solely motivated for charitable reasons—his consideration of others; for though he seemingly craves isolation, it does not mean he wishes to be totally alone. Whether he acknowledges it or not, the presence of other "bodies" is an imperative for living. And though he is a spiritless man, his instinct for survival remains.

In *The Pawnbroker*, "Wallant gives distilled examples of the human legacy and oppression," as David D. Galloway has pointed out (72). And he is absolutely correct. The structure of the novel is aligned to his dreams and to nearly every scene that precedes and follows each of his dreams. The entire novel focuses on Nazerman's reactions to his bitter, anguished memories. His associations with Ortiz and the other characters clarify his feelings—cold, brusque, biting, hate-filled—and they are catalytic. They are borne out of the deadly past, a past that will not leave him, not for one breathing moment. The entire novel is a depiction of the depths of evil of which man is capable. But it is also a novel about the restitution of the human spirit. The cost is high. It takes another man's self-sacrifice to restore the protagonist to the human family.

Even before his first dream, we read of his feelings about his surviving the Holocaust. He sardonically considers himself a miracle man in having escaped his seemingly destined death. He tells Jesus Ortiz, "It's a secret society I belong to . . . you have to be able to walk on water" (20). His bitter cynicism is now part of him. He can gain no respite. After his first dream we read: "The pawnbroker moaned in his sleep without waking. No one stirred in the house. They were used to his noisy sleep" (38). Neither waking nor sleeping can he escape the horror of the Holocaust. In answer to Tessie Mendel's question, "So what do we have in this life?" Nazerman answers, "We live and fight off the animals" (61-62). All people in his mind are equated with the exemplars of evil—the Nazis. Death for Sol Nazerman was "that old companion of his youth" (23). His life ended early in contrast to those outside the Holocaust, but he could not let go completely. His apprentice, Jesus Ortiz, tries to realize the cause of Nazerman's cold imperviousness to other human beings. "He looked at the blue numbers on his employer's arm and tried to work back from that cryptic sign to the figures that had made it" (75).

Nazerman's weak consent to Mrs. Harmon's philosophy "that what you bury might just as well stay dead" (77) is a subtle, ironic foreshadowing of his final realization that this belief is not true. He acknowledges that pain and anguish, just as joy and happiness, are fundamental facts of life.

Just before his second dream, we read of "the twenty-eighth of August . . . the anniversary of his family's death [which gives him] a vague sense of oppression" (91). "The first secret of his survival" (91) is to immerse himself entirely in the present "reality [which] consisted of the world within one's sight and smell and hearing. He communicated nothing; it was the secret of his survival" (91). He viewed life "with his unique spectacles on" (91), that is, within the purview of the Holocaust. It lay in the shadows of his mind—always—though he made great effort to "strangle [it] in the grip of his will" (98).

One of the most "distilled examples" (Galloway 72) of the depravity and desecration in the Holocaust occurs in Nazerman's second dream where we read of a man called Rubin, whose body Wallant describes as a "ragged bundle of blood and charred flesh . . . no longer Rubin or anything else" (*The Pawnbroker* 101). After his body has been charged by "the rattly crack of electricity" (101), it caused him to "pull away from the horrid life of the wires and then seize it tight in a lover's embrace" (101). This dream, together with his first dream, where he is helpless to rescue his son, which generates his wife's awful wrath, reverberates continuously throughout his nightmares. We read: "He saw his wife's grim face. She seemed to hate him" (38). He cannot escape this memory of his wife's "burning glass eye" (38) on him. His plea to her, "I can do nothing" (38) haunts him even now in the present. He lives a continuous nightmare. Self-blame and guilt, as well as hatred toward mankind, become indelible imprints on his soul.

After his second dream, his self-same reactions to the Holocaust are seen: "In some nameless graveyard of thought . . . he struggled to escape burial with things he had left behind forever" (11) or so he hoped. His bitterness toward all humankind is a continuous residual effect of the Holocaust. No one in the present reality is shielded from his withering scorn.

When he meets Goberman, a Jewish Nazi collaborator, we are again brought in direct contact with the Holocaust and the evils it engendered. We learn, as I have mentioned, of Goberman's survival at the price of yielding up his own family.

The enormity of Nazerman's torn spirit is made clear by Wallant in the pawnbroker's third dream: "However small a distortion they aimed at, it was far larger than they knew" (131). He cannot escape the pictures of his wife being raped before his very eyes nor the picture of his "child's dead body twisted on a monstrous hook which pierced it from behind and came out of the breast. He began screaming the screams of . . . unbearable size. His grief forced all of his blood out of its pores. . . . 'Naomi, Naomi Kinder, my baby, my baby'" (194). Such are some of the "distilled examples" (Galloway 72) that Wallant evokes in Nazerman's dreams. "A great and eternal sickness entered him" (*The Pawnbroker* 225).

After his third dream, his self-loathing and loathing for all men are emphasized. He scorns those who think of others, and he sides with those who can "project themselves into any act of brutality" (148). With these, he feels he "can hold his own" (148) because they, like him, are filled with hate. In his innermost thoughts, he can match their heinous acts.

Wallant foreshadows Nazerman's eventual change of heart when he mentions Nazerman's attempt to suppress the reality of his horrible past. "It was all right to scorn phantoms; but to pretend they did not exist was just foolhardy" (152).

After his fourth dream, he continues to abide by his decisions to submerge, as best he can, the reality of the Holocaust. "'I will sleep like the dead tonight,' he said longingly, but he slept like the living" (168). His nightmare will simply not go away. At the end of his fourth dream, he expresses his acid cynicism in humor of the blackest shade. In answer to the doctor's question concerning the dying Mendel's terrible appearance—"How did he get like that?:—Nazerman answers dryly: "A very bad accident of birth. He was in the camps" (191). After the fifth dream, he considers his own death and questions the mystery of life's meaning: "What is all this about then?" (194).

After the sixth dream, Wallant again reiterates Nazerman's contempt for humanity. In answer to Marilyn Birchfield's question: "Would you judge all people by the very worst you have seen?' 'I do,' he said coldly" (270). He attempts to deny the value of other people "by keeping his eyes . . . off their faces he was somehow able to conduct his business with a semblance of normality" (215).

After the seventh dream we read: "Tessie and even the corpse of Mendel seemed possessed of something vital and living while he himself stood without pain or grief, like a creature imbedded in plastic" (230). He has become almost inanimate. After the eighth dream, his despair is at its nadir. "'Today is the twenty eighth . . . my anniversary.' One could only die once. He had been extinct a long time" (249).

Thus Wallant voices his opinion on Nazerman's existence—a truly pathetic one. Even the evil Murillo recognizes Nazerman's sorry condition: "I believe there is no point in killing you" (261). And a little later: "He tried to remember a time when he had been alive but failed miserably [and] life fell like a shadow on his soul" (264-265). But at this darkest moment of his existence, Ortiz acts as a sacrifice for the pawnbroker, and by doing so, activates Nazerman's long dormant conscience, making him acknowledge finally the value of another. It is Ortiz's act that "made him insist on even the myriad varieties of pain he had endured . . . everything he had thought he had conquered rose up from its sham death and fell upon him" (272).

After his final dream, he awakens to the reality of love, the recognition of brotherhood, of love in the concrete. In speaking to his nephew, he says, "I need you to help me. I have no one" (275). He then decides to confront his abortive attempts to live in the pain engendered by the Holocaust: "He found the dream to be oddly without the usual horror and yet possessed of the greatest sadness he had ever experienced" (275). "'I am all right now.'" (276). "He began to cry . . . for all the dead now [and] his tears continued . . ., helpless, wretched, strangely proud" (278)—"strangely proud" because in his act of self-sacrifice, Ortiz had made him realize that others recognized him as a person of value, not as a subhuman creature. He realized at the end there are not only Nazis, but people like Ortiz, who he himself had said was incapable "of certain horrors" (11). He now knows love is the difference; some exemplify it, others deny it.

Descriptions of Nazerman's dreams themselves add further credence to the fact that the Holocaust is the primary, pervasive subject of *The Pawnbroker*—that, and the protagonist's reactions to it. Some of the more graphic language Wallant uses in describing Nazerman's dreams attest to the fact that the novel hinges on this most abominable event. In dream one, Wallant writes of the pawnbroker's helplessness before his son's pleas: "I'm slipping in it, Daddy, in the dirty stuff" (37) to which Nazerman replies, "I am helpless, do you hear?" (38). In dream two, there is no life above or below the earth: "The dogs brayed in the hot light. The air was emptied of birds and insects by the loud voices of the dogs, and the prisoners stood like shades, arrested on their shuffling journey to hell" (100). In this same dream, we read: "Rubin was screaming, one shining red figure of blood, only his mouth definable in all the torn body, and that so vivid because it framed the scream. Everything else was dust white, the dark figures of the guards and the dogs overladen with a clouded, powdered white. Only Rubin had immense color . . . a great crimson font that demeaned the whole day" (101).

In dream four, we read of his wife's degradation and his reaction to it: "Her face turned the color of calcimine, the texture of some powdery substance that could crumble at a touch. . . . She endured the zenith of her agony and was able to pass through it. Until finally she was able to award him the tears of forgiveness. But he was not worthy of her award and took the infinitely meaner triumph of blindness. . . . He no longer had to share the obscene experience with her. He went a step further toward the empty blackness of animal relief" (169). Finally in dream seven we read: "The smell of burning flesh entered him" (225). Is it no wonder his spirit was filled with hatred toward all mankind until he sees there are people like "my Ortiz" (147).

It appears then that Mr. Wallant in no way "trivializes" (Berger 165) the Holocaust, but as Harold Ribalow has said, "I don't know how much Ed Wallant considered himself a Jewish writer. Only truth has the curious facility of transcending all backgrounds and taking on that marvelous flexibility which gives to each reader his own personal application of the truth involved" (10). It seems the ugly truth of the Holocaust permeates every page of *The Pawnbroker*.

Chapter 4

Methods of Presentation I
Allegory—Parables—Biblical Allusions

Parallel methods of presentation in their evocation of theme is another vital factor that conjoins Wallant and O'Connor, and one of the chief literary strands that fuses the two together is their pronounced use of allegory. In reviewing Wallant's fiction, Thomas M. Lorch thinks that "*The Pawnbroker* . . . contains a vein of allegory, both in its settings and in its character relationships" (Lorch 81b). He contends that "its primary setting, the pawnshop, represents various aspects of Western civilization. It reveals the underside of man's dependence on things, both [in] the pathos of his efforts to protect himself with things and immense weight of things crushing in upon him" (82). Lorch also thinks Wallant "employs the pawnshop to criticize materialism and the capital system itself and [that] the nature of the pawning transaction suggests that the Western economic system is based on exploitation and degradation. . . . Money [he believes] . . . exerts considerable force in the novel . . . yet in spite of all this, things still have only the value people give them, and Sol's transactions retain a human dimension. This dimension [Lorch maintains] derives from the customer's humanity and his own. . . . Both the tightly woven structure and the allegorical dimension of *The Pawnbroker* are manifested in the character relationships and directly or indirectly all these relationships focus on Sol Nazerman and their allegorical dimension derives from the fact that most dramatize various facets of Sol's inner life" (82). "This [according to Lorch] is the type of allegory defined by C. S. Lewis in *The Allegory of Love,* in which individual characters represent distinct inner forces and the conflict between these characters on the literal level portrays inner conflicts" (Lorch 71b).

In his novels, "Wallant's major theme [is] the dilemma of the individual faced with the problem of evil. [His] primary interest [is] the problem of evil" (Lorch 78). It is obvious that much the same can be said of O'Connor's primary theme with her continued stress on the conflict between good and evil in all her writings. In *The Pawnbroker*, Sol's efforts to reject his past and to repress his humanity are both futile and harmful. . . . His agonizing recovery begins when he realized that his collaboration with Murillo is a form of complicity" (83). This would make him an equal to Goberman, the hypocrite he hates. His repentance is generated by two causes—his desire to break relations with evil itself in the person of Murillo, but it is also prompted [as mentioned] by his not wishing to be compared to Goberman. The comparison is too invidious for his ego to bear. It is in this respect his rejection of Murillo is less altruistic than it appears. His egocentricity detracts to a slight degree from the moral nature of his act.

Lorch also argues persuasively that it is Nazerman's "relationship with his assistant Jesus Ortiz [that] emerges as the richest and most intimate in the novel. [Lorch thinks] neither understands what is happening and [that] both resist it. [He sees] Jesus as the primary agent of Sol's rebirth, [and that his] name and the religious imagery . . . are too insistent to be ignored. [Lorch also thinks that] Jesus functions as another aspect of Sol's inner life, and the facet of personality he most accentuates is the capacity for love and sacrifice. [He feels that] Wallant depicts Jesus and Sol as very much alike" (83-84). It seems that Sol and Jesus are more than very much alike when one considers the recognizable traits and attitudes that link the two. It is, in fact, difficult not to see them as doubles. As counterparts of each other, they complement each other.

Lorch's interpretation appears quite apt. What is pronounced in *The Pawnbroker* are the subtle, alternating roles that Ortiz and Sol play in their pilgrimage to their ultimate destiny. Each, at one time or another, may indeed be seen as an image of the Christ Himself; yet, at other times, as the picture of the anti Christ. Nazerman's attitude makes a strong case for his resemblance to the sardonic Satanic figure: "Trace anything far enough and it leads to filth. Even rescuing angels must have some grime on their wings" (6). In his self-pity, he is immune to the anguish of others. "His shop creaked with the burden of other people's sorrows [yet] he abided, indifferent to their sorrows after his own trial"

(25). Indeed, he considers his tragic customers "assailants" (47), disturbing to his quest for privacy. He is continually bent on isolating himself from others. There are moments, however, when "for some unknown reason" (48), he exhibits minute signs of goodness, as in his tolerating of the pathetic George Smith. We read, "He gave the poor beast a few minutes of talk [and] in spite of everything, their talk created a small, faintly warming buzz in the pawnshop [and] the burned spirit of the colored man was warmed in the bright myriad reflections of the names and words and possibly in some lesser, more remote way in the consciousness of the rock-colored pawnbroker" (50). But Nazerman's consideration for Smith's feelings do not spring from a full blown generosity of spirit. "He just didn't have the courage yet to humiliate him and drive him away as he wanted to" (107). His generosity is tainted by thoughts of self, just as his act of "redemption" was in breaking his relationship with Murillo.

The symbolic reference to the pawnbroker's assistant as Christ-like in aspect is rendered dramatically when Ortiz succeeds in performing the ultimate Christ-like act—sacrificing his life for the sake of another. It is Ortiz's goal to know the mystery of Sol's being, that "buried treasure" (21) of his being. Under the spell of Nazerman's mysterious heritage, Ortiz becomes "involved in an odd current of emotions, softened and blinded and bound . . . and what Ortiz aspired to, he sensed in the pawnbroker even though he did not recognize the shape of his aspiration. He sensed without knowledge that a deep hollow in him [was] filled with the pawnbroker's voice" (180). What this aspiration is, is finally made concrete, given vital form in Ortiz's act of self-renunciation. This culminating act specifies that unknownst to Nazerman himself, there lay the seed of goodness in him, a goodness in spirit that refused to be extinguished. What may appear surprising about Ortiz's final act relates to his earlier scoffing at the "myth" (96) of the crucified Savior. "He went to the Catholic Church [and] knelt without prayer before the Crucifix" (9), and a bit later, "It was a fairy tale [and he] wondered why he allowed himself obeisance to it" (238). He figured "a white Jesus couldn't know the half of it" (238) With smugness, he vents his antipathy toward the Savior.

And though Ortiz resists the truth of the cross, or as he terms it, the "myth" (96) of the cross, there was something in or about it that "strangely made him feel the anguish of love" (10). Both his "teacher" (116), Sol Nazerman, and his "lover" (236), Mabel Wheatley, feel the good that lay dormant within Ortiz's anguished spirit. Mabel "yearned toward some odd bright cleanliness she imagined in him. Half-consciously she saw a hope of escape [from her life of prostitution] in him" (65).

In attempting to discover the mystery of the pawnbroker's spirit, Ortiz felt that "many things of great significance just lay in the quality of [his] voice. . . . Horror and exultation seemed to reside in the pawnbroker's mysterious history" (75). In moving toward the answer to Nazerman's elusive spirit, the foreshadowing of Ortiz's final fate is presented in undeniably religious terms: "Ortiz imagined himself approaching a great light in the earth, filled with an immense trembling excitement, not knowing the source of the light, moving toward it and wondering whether it would be fearsome or exulting" (71). The connection made here links Nazerman's "mysterious history" (72) to the "great light" (71). In Nazerman's history, there is both "horror and exultation—horror in his pain-filled experience of the Holocaust, yet exultation in his forthcoming dramatic transformation after Ortiz's sacrifice. In the reference to "the great light," there is found fear or exultation. In his sacrificial act, Ortiz reveals dramatically that fear is overcome by joy; his act implies his "exultation" at overcoming his fear and being rewarded with joyful, open arms by the "great light" (71).

Nazerman's reaction to Ortiz's sacrifice is resonant with religious symbolism, in the same, if not greater degree than Ortiz's. In beholding the dying Ortiz, we read of Nazerman: "His body felt full of the flow of some great wound. A rush and a torment burned him. He felt naked and flayed and he hung over the dying youth like a frayed canopy" (272). Ortiz's mother's cries fill "the pawnbroker's ears . . . dragging him back to the sea of tears he had thought to escape. . . . All his anesthetic numbness left him. He became terrified of the touch of air on the raw wounds and again the questions: What was this great agonizing sensitivity and what was it for? Love?" (272). The lingering effects of his self-inflicted isolation make him even in trauma, question the value of love: "Oh no, not love? For whom?" (273). He finds his answer through feeling—that part of man he had attempted to imprison. He begins "to cry . . . blinded by his weeping . . . he thudded into people and felt them and took into himself their peculiar odors of sweat and breath or dirt and hair, the smell of the great mortal decay that was living because it was dying, and when he tried to wipe his eyes, indeed, cleared them momentarily, he saw the ineffable marvel of their eyes and skins" (278). He has awakened to humanity, been transformed from a death-in-life creature to a man.

From these passages it may be inferred that both Ortiz and Nazerman may be viewed as the Christ Himself and as the anti-Christ; Ortiz, as a Christ figure, is an "unfathomable lover" (72) of man. His own mother conjures up the image of Mary, the Mother of the Savior, by her wailing sorrow: "Jesus, Jesus, is it my Jesus?" (272). Yet in a seeming reciprocity of roles, the pawnbroker himself seems to figure forth this very same savior. This parallel is given credence by Ortiz whose self-sacrifice for his "master" (51) makes him "glimpse again the figure of a holy man, awkwardly transfixed on a cross, a man with blue, cryptic numbers on his arm" (247) whereas earlier Ortiz had fixated on that very idea. "He [Christ crucified] was a Jew, like the pawnbroker. Wouldn't everybody be surprised to see Sol Nazerman up there?" (238). In answer to his belief that "nothing in this world makes sense" (238), Ortiz finds an answer in the mystery attached to the pawnbroker's spirit. This world of sense provides him with no answers; his act at the end is generated by the spirit of love that lay dormant in Nazerman's soul. Ortiz's imagining of Nazerman on the cross is strengthened by the words applied earlier to him as one whose figure contained all elements of something "majestic and tragic" (257) and who seems to see himself as one on whom "all were making profit . . . they found ease from their individual pains at the sight of his great aggregate of pains, they looked at the stock of the store and saw it all as a tremendous weight on him and that seemed to awe them too, for as they added their own small item, it was as though they piled on weight to prove his immense power, so that even some went out laughing, having left him a piece of their pain" (257). So, as "doubles" of the Savior, both men seem to have listened "to some third person" (180), the true living Lord who never succumbed to the onerous cancer of self-pity.

As Lorch has said, Sol Nazerman's "relationship with his assistant Jesus Ortiz . . . emerges as the richest and most intimate in the novel" (83). This richness and intimacy is brought about by the complexity of the relationship between the two, which alternates between feelings that engender both hatred and love. And though we witness Nazerman's movement toward self-discovery, it seems never completely realized by himself. This very human, complex man assumes at different times the faces of both the major and the minor characters: Goberman, Robinson, Murillo, and especially, as we have noted, Ortiz.

In Nazerman's detestation of Goberman, he resembles Goberman who cannot face the truth that he betrayed his own family that he might live. Though Nazerman did not betray his family, his helping the Nazis pile up the bodies of his fellow Jews impinged on his conscience, making him feel in some way a collaborator in evil. Wallant's conclusion is that Nazerman, although accepting the pain of his calculated conduct toward others, has become in no way happy "like a martyr" (279). He knows his ego is involved in his redemptive act.

Another example of Nazerman's "self-inflicted blindness" (214) is his inability to see any connection between himself and Robinson, the cold, vengeful killer, who, like Nazerman, "could recall every day spent in prison . . . yet had no emotional recall of any of it" (201). Though Nazerman in his anguish does have "emotional recall" of the Holocaust, he tries with acute, desperate consciousness to submerge it. The past, for both men, bred anger and hatred and in this negative respect, they are brothers.

Murillo, Nazerman's silent partner in the pawnshop, upon whose good will Nazerman depends for this livelihood, is another pathetic character whom the pawnbroker resembles. Just as Nazerman begrudges his time to pain-filled souls like George Smith, so Murillo begrudges his time to listen to the pawnbroker's cries, and just as Nazerman speaks to his customers in cold, indifferent tones, so too does Murillo in his exchanges with the pawnbroker. His matter-of-fact answers flatly reject any solicitations: "His voice came like the one that gives the time and the weather: 'I expect you at ten fifteen tonight, punctual, understand?'" (151). He scoffs at Nazerman's ignorance of the ill-gained money that keeps him in business. Wallant writes of the penalty the pawnbroker must pay in persisting to live in his world where self-investigation is anathema. "It was all right to scorn phantoms, but to pretend they did not exist was just foolhardy" (152). The pawnbroker's late concession to reality is one that leaves him forever immersed in wallowing self-pity: "I want only to be left alone" (165). His pretensions continue to imprison him within himself.

But the primary obstacle to Nazerman's inability to see himself is his inability to see the intimate connection between Ortiz and himself. It may be seen that they are mystically linked. Like Nazerman, Ortiz is self-concerned: "'I figure my plans for me alone'" (66). And, like Nazerman, he has emotional scars. "Mabel had always been afraid to ask Jesus what had happened to him, well aware of his strange inexplicable sore sports"

Methods of Presentation I 35

(5). In what might be termed a mystical-physical relationship, Nazerman and Ortiz are very much alike. Of Ortiz we read, "He knows his body exists but feels bodiless" (153). And although he curses the elusiveness of Nazerman's spirit, he, himself, is just as elusive. No one really knows him—his own mother, his lover Mabel; his partners in crime, Buck White, Tangee, and Robinson: and certainly not Nazerman. Wallant writes, "They were a strangely matched team [who] felt crowded by the smells of the poorly washed peoples, of cheaply perfumed bodies of the poverty-stricken, of the diseased" (105). Nazerman admits that Ortiz is a mystery to him. "I have a strange assistant, my Jesus Ortiz. I understand him as little as he does me" (147).

Under Nazerman's tutelage Ortiz becomes the pawnbroker's shadow, his alter-ego. "He was clever, able to deal well enough with both his customers and those the pawnbroker almost made disastrous deals with" (216). Both get agitated at the least sign of vulnerability. After feeling a momentary sadness for Nazerman's apparent plight, "An outrage hits him. . . . 'all this crap got to end,' he savaged silently" (217). The "murderous pity" (220) in his eyes at the sight of Nazerman's seeming breakdown is filled with invidious self-indulgence. He relishes his anger. This same inner rage fills Nazerman's being in his encounter with George Smith, whom he had condescendingly suffered on several occasions. His rage at his own softness in putting up with Smith finally breaks out: "Go away, I cannot be bothered with all you crazy . . . all you animals . . . your filth" (221). His rage, like Ortiz's is bolstered by his self-indulgent spirit. As the novel reaches its climax, the two are "alone" (220); they are separated from each other by a wall of "silence" (220).

Ortiz gradually becomes as isolated as the pawnbroker. "He felt himself to be advancing toward a strange and icy outpost, more remote than anything he had experienced before" (233). And just as Nazerman had rejected his "lover" Tessie's pain, so too Ortiz rejects his lover Mabel's: "He couldn't see Mabel's pain, wouldn't have seen it even if he been looking in her direction, even if it had been as bright as day" (236). And like Nazerman, he gives his pain priority over everyone else's. Looking up to the crucified Christ, he says, "Oh man you don't know the half of it, it's too complicated for you" (238). This outburst is equal in its egocentricity to Nazerman's defense of himself. When he speaks to Marilyn Birchfield, whose world of loneliness as a single woman, living in a cold, crowded metropolis, is met with fortitude and courage, we read of Nazerman's excuse for his anti-social behavior: "My world is so different in scale that its emotions bear no resemblance to yours" (146). This remark is jarring in its effect, for though his pain has been fostered by horrific events, which lie beyond the imagination of Ms. Birchfield's world, it belittles the woman's inherent value as a human being, one capable of feeling her own unique pain. His immersion into the self continues to fester and to grow.

At the end of the novel, Ortiz begins to feel "the icy dart of disaster" (247). Both men find themselves bound in a dark lit chamber of spirit. And what had seemed impossible to the tormented pawnbroker, now becomes possible: "Above him the footsteps of his assistant in the loft creaked and thudded as though the slender figure moved under a burden heavier than himself" (264).

In what might be termed the good side of the similitude, neither man is enamored of his occupation. In Nazerman's case, we read: "When he got to the store, he could not resist a grimace at the sight of the three gilded balls hanging over the doorway. It was no more than a joke in rather poor taste that had led to this" (6). In Ortiz's case, he felt a "strange dedication to the job that his sense of logic told him was a fool's vocation" (9). And both men exhibit momentary pangs of conscience: "They were riven by the complexity, the intricacy of the tools of people's survival, and each in his own unthinking way, responded to a tiny, sad abrasion in his spirit. Each of them pitied, without knowing he pitied, the pathetic paraphernalia with which humans made walls" (111).

In referring back to the idea that Nazerman and Ortiz may be pictured as "doubles," as intimate counterparts of each other, this connection is in evidence even in the physical sense. Under Nazerman's guidance, Ortiz becomes "facile and cool and clever" (216) in his dealings with customers as Nazerman had been—always "calm, inscrutable, giving nothing for nothing" (113). Both feel the security the pawnshop offers them. As the pawnbroker went "behind the part of the counter where the barbed wire was, he felt sure of himself there" (182). In Ortiz's case, his apprenticeship with Sol made him feel important. He thought "that business made him solid . . . like a king" (51). And both see money as a supreme priority. There was in Nazerman something Ortiz wished "to possess [and for this something]. . . he had only the simple words for material things: money, a business, a name" (258). He thinks about money and the power of business, just as Nazerman does, who "puts himself to sleep by calculating the compound interest in savings" (130). And like the pawnbroker, Ortiz trusts no one.

Wallant calls them "a strangely matched team" (105). In the beginning, Ortiz considers Nazerman his teacher, whereas at the end, he is termed the pawnbroker's "enigmatic rescuer" (217). It is Ortiz who seeks to possess Nazerman's "secret of success" (51-52), and the pawnbroker admits to being, perhaps without too much thought, the possessor of his "strange assistant," calling him at one point "My Jesus Ortiz" (147). At the novel's end, Wallant terms Nazerman's loss of Ortiz, the loss of one irreplaceable negro" (278). For the pawnbroker, ironically, this loss is in reality his greatest gain, for he has his life restored by Ortiz's ultimate sacrifice.

As mentioned earlier, Nazerman's discovery of self appears never fully realized, but his heretofore dominant emotion of hate, graphically demonstrated in his excoriation of Goberman, has been transcended by his heartfelt love for his fellow man, represented by Ortiz. He no longer "thinks the worst of everyone" (45). This breakthrough, in itself, is a major step toward his salvation. Whether he thinks like Marilyn Birchfield that there is "hope for everyone" (145) is a moot question. It is for this reason *The Pawnbroker* may be considered a novel of transformation rather than conversion. Nazerman's change in character signifies a change of heart, which is indeed no small accomplishment.

In the case of Flannery O'Connor, Thomas Lorch also notes an allegorical turn. He says: "In her efforts to portray the 'experience of mystery' [O'Connor was] led . . . quite naturally to allegory" (Lorch 69a). He thinks that "in both theme and technique, *Wise Blood* resembles John Bunyan's *Pilgrim's Progress*. . . . Like Christian, Haze is on a quest for God. . . . He sleeps with Mrs. Watts who represents the flesh [and] . . . he buys a car . . . to escape from religion, [but] the Essex . . . cannot take him on a spiritual journey [and] when he finally puts on his mother's glasses, he begins to see the perversion of his ways and [he] turns toward true belief" (Lorch 70a). Lorch concludes that it is in this novel that "Miss O'Connor . . . employs the traditional Christian allegory which alone gives meaning to Haze's actions and his quest" (71).

Wise Blood may then be seen as a novel allegorical in nature, in that nearly every action, every object, every character, either good or evil, is imbued with symbolically laden intent. The novel focuses on a universal theme—the ongoing conflict in man between choosing good or evil. It is a conflict that permits no peace of mind, a conflict that rends and burns man's very soul until he acts with finality—deciding with no reservations—on choosing the good or evil. Whichever he chooses will lead him to his final destiny, a destiny freely chosen. Wallant's concerns are parallel to those of O'Connor in this respect. His protagonists choose for themselves their final destiny after much soul-searching.

Wallant's *The Children at the Gate* has also been commended for "the skill, richness, and allegorical depth which [the novelist] exhibited in it" (Lorch 84b). Lorch finds "the allegorical dimension . . . grows out of Angelo's experiences at the hospital [and] though less successful than the pawnshop as an image of Western civilization, the hospital is an effective image of the mind. . . . [He thinks] Lebedov is an almost allegorical figure of desire . . . 'I want' . . . [and that] Sammy is . . . the sole agent of Angelo's rebirth [because he] acts as a true guide. He examines Angelo like a judging but merciful God, and despite Angelo's resistance, develops a psychic, almost mystical power over him. [He] also functions as Angelo's alter-ego, as a manifestation of Angelo's hitherto suppressed but gradually emerging true self. [Lorch concludes rightly that] . . . Sammy remains a rich, extraordinary fictional figure" (85-87).

In contrast to Sammy's integrity, Angelo, though touched by Lebedov's cries of contrition, had fought up through the unaccustomed pity that had formed" (*The Children at the Gate* 106) in him, and he attempts to attribute Lebedov's actions to strictly biological causes: "Some kind of brain damage" (110). But when McKenna, the autopsy technician, tries to support his conclusion, he becomes enraged, knowing intuitively that his dependency on man's biological make-up as a catalyst for all his actions is meaningless. "Angelo snarled suddenly, 'Stop bending my goddam ear'" (110).

Unlike Angelo, Sammy does not dissimulate. He knows and admits that he, like Lebedov and all men, is vulnerable to crimes of passion: "Maybe now it's Lebedov, but during that time when I felt it was me . . . I think how nice it would be if Einstein could see it and make it clear. But I don't think it's possible, I think that only dreykops like me, dopes like me, see these things" (120). Here faith in mystery contends with reason in seeking the truth. In the scene where love appears triumphant over death, Angelo, the science advocate, remains ignorant about the beneficent effects of love. The dying Sydney's words to his loving wife Hetty—"I don't need anyone but you" (126)—are met by Angelo's reaction, "What's the point?" (126), which signifies the petrified grip of practicality that pervades his being. In answer to Angelo's protest to Sammy—"You don't have to smell their breath or touch their skin" (127) to know others. [Sammy retorts:] "For some like you, that's what you have to do" (127).

Angelo's contrast to Sammy lies in his attitude toward life, toward the meaning of man's existence. Angelo, as a firm ally of the practical, of the reasonable—"He fixed hard on what was" (55)—also acknowledges as a realist the flaws in himself. He knows he has weaknesses and needs, but he believes he can "expect nothing" (76) from life. He thinks he knows more about man's potential for evil than the old nun "with only her little black book of fairy tales to guide her" (85). He disdains man's animal nature and feels above all crimes of passion. He considers other people soulless as flowers: "Things grow, just to be cut, to wither and die . . . like blown seeds in a random world" (101). He is emphatic in denying man's unique place in creation. "What's so special about us?" (121). Life, he thinks is "an accident, things happen for no reason. . . . Nothing is anybody's fault" (167); he thus absolves himself from any personal faults.

But Sammy does not leave him alone. He antagonizes him with a "face long and pearly and a tall narrow white shape" (29); he continuously haunts Angelo with probing questions—"Do you know where you're going?" (29)—with jokes and stories, which, for the logical Angelo, have no reasoned pattern. In answer to Angelo's question, "Where'd you come from?" (35), Sammy answers vaguely, "Oh, all over" (35). He says he is "Jewish—not pushy or loud [and that as an orderly he has] worked Jewish, Catholic, Protestant, Quaker [and] non-sectarian" (35) hospitals and that he is "hard-working, honest, respectful and efficient" (35). He reviles Angelo's practical bent, referring to him as "a regular scientist" (55), and he rebukes his nihilism in sardonic tones: "Everything is nothing" (56). In contrast to Angelo, who believes solely in "facts" (71), Sammy holds that "Nothing is like it looks" (66). He mocks Angelo's attempts to know how the world works: "You're a scientist, you got all this figured out" (69). In anger, Angelo snarls at Sammy's beguiling composure: "Who the hell do you think you are?" (129), to which Sammy answers with a question and an answer which touches the very core of Angelo's beliefs about humanity: "Who is anyone? That's what you should have been asking all along" (129). Angelo's philosophy that man is simply just another physical, animate creature who is born, lives, and dies precludes any further thought on his side to see what Sammy is postulating. It is only after Sammy's death that Angelo is finally able to leave his isolated world where he equates everything with nothing.

Sammy appears a Christ-like figure who can see into people's hearts: "His white face incredibly earnest; 'It's like I can see their nerves'" (37). He tells Angelo he has suffered and will continue to do so: "Don't worry about me. I've been around" (38). Like Jesus' parables, his "stories" mesmerize his listeners. He "leads his listeners' attention as a conductor leads his musicians" (58). His stories bring peace to the tormented Lebedov and the effeminate Howard Miller. "Lebedov sat nodding and moving his hands, his bestial face was animated; his eyes gleamed.... Howard Miller's face stopped twitching, became almost sleepy and still [and] ... Angelo was appalled at his own helplessness" (58) before him. Sammy's voice brings comfort to the afflicted. Angelo hears "the high voice answer with a queer amused-sounding tenderness, 'Okay friend, it's all right. Sammy's coming. Shhh, not so loud'" (58). As Christ became man's servant, so too does Sammy.

After trying to sell the people on the idea of forgiveness, he is beaten and battered, yet is Christ-like in aspect, in his persecution. "His eyes were tranquil under the mask of tragedy" (149). The tragedy in Sammy's mind was not that he had suffered but that his pleas for forgiveness on man's part had fallen on hardened hearts. He tells Angelo, "People just don't realize.... They get deeper and deeper in with their words. But they don't know.... They hide the earth from themselves with steel and formica so that they can forget they're going to be buried in dirt. What they need is a big, big tremendous joke to make them see the one little thing ... that.... How can they.... No, but they got to remember Lebedov. He's a human—that's all there should be. There shouldn't be anything but people on the earth. If we become buried in this world and forget to forgive and love, as we are meant to, if we forget we all die, what is the good of all our adulation of formica and steel" (150). The essence of Sammy's homily is: In our denigration of our fellow-sinner, we denigrate ourselves.

Sammy's presence (much like O'Connor's Bishop) effects diverse reactions. Some welcome him whereas others reject him. "All around the tall, gangly figure, the patients exuded an atmosphere of anger and ecstasy" (51). Sammy believes in brotherhood and the communion of all men—"We all have to hold hands in the dark" (16)—and he assumes a Christ-like posture just before his death. "His hands were out, palms upward" (170), just as the statue of Jesus is pictured earlier. "Jesus held his hands out as though for alms" (20). We know neither Sammy nor the Lord was interested in money. It seems evident from these allusions that Wallant figures forth a Jewish orderly filled with the compassionate and loving spirit of man's true Savior.

In their spiritual kinship, both O'Connor and Wallant make frequent allusions to the Old and the New Testaments. On Wallant's fiction, Harold U. Ribalow has noted that "Wallant has dealt with the difficult matter of man communicating with his fellow. His books are full of pain and sadness, of agony and God, of Jews and Christians, disturbed and seeking. [With his fiction] he has left us books . . . that help us to understand our neighbors, our fellow Jews and some of the problems faced by contemporary man" (327). God, in Wallant's novels, is a mysterious, pivotal presence. In his fiction there is a "universalized but essentially Hebraic prophetic strain that underlies Wallant's own commitment to human survival, universal kinship, and irrepressible faith [that] pulses throughout his works" (Marovitz 173). Wallant "had an idea [according to Marcus Klein] which must be called religious [but which leads to] a dismissal of (Jewish) culture" (Klein 240). And though Marovitz has noted "the Hebraic prophetic strain" in Wallant inherent in his religious vision, he goes even further by saying that "despite many overt references to Judaism and Christianity in his fiction . . . formal religion has much less effect over the lives and actions of Wallant's characters than love and the universal spirit. . . . Despite clear religious affiliations in all four novels, the doctrines of neither Catholicism nor Judaism determine the attitudes and behavior of the major characters" (Marovitz 180).

William V. Davis argues for "a synthesis of Christian and Jewish themes [in Wallant]. [He thinks] . . . through his superimposition of a Christian set of symbols and metaphors on the Jewish base of his characters and setting, Wallace has created a new genre" (98). Davis suggests that Sugarman in *The Tenants of Moonbloom* "precedes Moonbloom and gives him his direction. He may therefore be considered in line with the Biblical parallels: the John the Baptist figure or the Deutero-Isaiah figure" (Davis 104).

In seeing Wallant's characters motivated by universal love rather than by any adherence to "formal religion," Marovitz says that "the tie that binds the Hebrew prophets specifically to Yahweh is clear and distinct, whereas Sammy's prophetic utterances transcend the barriers of doctrine and creed by which one religion is separated from another. [Wallant, he says] is instead a prophet of universal spiritual truth and of love. . . . Sammy illustrates his message as Jesus did through actions and parables. It takes time, but finally his words have the same dynamic effect on Angelo as those of Jesus did on his disciples and the many believers that have followed him since then" (Marovitz 181). Marovitz thinks Wallant's "voice . . . echoes through his fiction urging us . . . to a greater commitment to our uniquely human capacity for humility, wonder and spiritual communion" (182). Marcus Klein agrees with this idea expressed in Wallant of a "spiritual communion" that brings all men together. He argues that Wallant's "purpose . . . was to locate an ordinary, precisely middling ground of reality [where] the Jew . . . is everybody" (Klein 240, 232). This reality of inclusiveness is what Davis called Wallant's aim at "a synthesis of Christian and Jewish themes" (Davis 98).

Nicholas Ayo also notes what other critics have that Wallant's "male protagonists such as Sammy, Jesus, and Norman would qualify as sinner-saints [and] the details of their life . . . invite comparison with Jesus of Nazareth, even if Wallant had not left a trail of lightly veiled allegory and even direct references to the Cross" (91). Ayo also notes that even "for the non-believer, the references to the gospel operate at least on the level of allusion to a well-known and powerful myth of sacrifice and rebirth. [Ayo also adds that] Wallant's Christ figures primarily emphasize the characteristics of a victim. Both Jesus and Sammy are fatherless, and they both lay down their life for someone else. [Ortiz's] prayer the night before he is shot makes reference to Christ as a negro. And Sammy, the victim in the extreme, takes upon himself the sins of the world. Sammy's life and death suggest elaborate gospel parallels. He is the most obvious Christ figure, or sinner-saint, or victim-hero among Wallant's characters. From the entomology of his name, "anointed with the Lord," to the spear in his heart at his death, [his] life has further meaning. . . . The bread and wine rituals with Angelo in the solarium become a mystical liturgy. Sammy jokes about walking on water, but he lives in order to minister to the suffering of others. Both the sacred and the profane, both the sacred heart and the secular heart, can be viewed as embodiments of a common ground, the human condition" (Ayo 86, 90-93).

What appears to be a slight point of irony in viewing the allusions to the Bible in each writer's work is that Wallant, a Jew, seems to stress allusions to the New Testament, whereas O'Connor, a Catholic, "reflects the influence of the Old Testament prophets in her voice and vision" (Rabasca 3963a). Conchita Rabasca notes that "the prophets [of the Old Testament and in O'Connor's fiction] make a distinction between finite and transcendent reality and assume the presence of a supernatural world within the natural. [Rabasca argues that] both [the Old Testament and O'Connor's fiction] are structured around the archetype of spiritual exile, epiphany and journey home" (3963a). She also notes that "in both literatures, the journey out of exile is often precipitated by violence" (3963a). She concludes by saying, "And in both [literatures] a way is offered for experiencing the mystery of revelation that leads to a confrontation with a loving God. [And] both hold up to the light the moral failings of their societies and point the way to redemption" (3963a).

It appears then many of these key concepts form another link between Wallant and O'Connor, because these same ideas are very much in evidence in Wallant's novels. For example, is not the idea of witnessing "the supernatural in the natural" also found in Wallant's *The Human Season*, especially in the scene where Joe Berman, as a young boy, and his revered father view the river and in its "singing" hear the voice of God? Wallant and O'Connor seem to work in tandem from every standpoint, be it in structure or in content.

In a study she makes of Flannery O'Connor, Janet M. Gallagher notes "a nearly biblical third person narrative in *The Violent Bear It Away* [in which O'Connor alludes to] 2 Samuel 9-20 [which] encourages the reader to experience its theology of a hidden God, who nevertheless is active in history" (1221a). In Wallant, this concept of a "hidden God . . . active in history" is illustrated prominently in *The Human Season*, where the invisible God jolts Berman into realizing and accepting the fact that man must die in God's time, not in man's. Gallagher contends that "what *The Violent Bear It Away* has in common with 2 Samuel 9-20 is an emphasis upon the difficult [in] knowing" (1221a).

This concept about "difficult knowing" as a significant theme is also noted by Sister N. Bernetta Quinn, O.S.F., who says O'Connor's "characters . . . do for reality what the Biblical prophets did: impart a fuller significance to what everyone experiences. [She also notes that O'Connor] concentrates on the less publicized prophets (Amos, Osee, Jonah and Obadiah) who endeavored to make their contemporaries see how far they were departing from what God wanted" (142).

Preston Browning, Jr., cites O'Connor's specific use in "Parker's Back" of "the Old Testament Obadiah [who] was a sixth century prophet, who, in a vision, predicted the destruction that would befall Edom for her unrighteousness" (Browning 528). Browning notes that "the subject of ["Parker's Back" appears to be] the awakening to the awe-ful presence of the numinous in one who had beforehand been as insensitive as stone, as ordinary as a loaf of bread" (*Complete Stories* 513). Browning continues: "The failure to understand himself is patently a failure to understand the restlessness, the eternal dissatisfaction that plagues him. [Parker is] soon to discover that he is, in truth, a blind boy. . . . The Byzantine Christ, from which a sense of the numinous streams forth is [his] inevitable choice. . . . He dimly perceives the 'God above' from whom he [has been] fleeing and toward whom he is driven throughout the story" (528-530). Browning adds that in "Parker's Back," reluctant prophet that he is, Parker makes one final attempt to escape his destiny" (530). This same reluctancy is also quite evident in Wallant's Norman Moonbloom, who did everything he could to avoid finding mystery in his own being.

In addition to her allusions to the Old Testament, O'Connor "also makes biblical allusions to the New Testament, specifically to Matthew 11 . . . in *The Vision Bear it Away*. [O'Connor uses the first twelve verses of Matthew to determine form and meaning in the novel. . . . She uses scripture (therefore) . . . as an ordering device. . . .] Chapters 10 through 12 focus upon [Tarwater's] mission undertaken in emulation of John the Baptist. [And] when Christ became real for him, and because of the recalcitrance of the secular city to repent, his prophetic mission will always be violent, and he himself will be a violent protagonist who through his zealousness can win heaven not only for himself but for those who learn repentance" (Muller 20-21, 24).

Clinton Trowbridge notes that it is Tarwater's "spiritual hunger" that drove him to his destined vocation. He says that in *The Violent Bear It Away*, O'Connor "wove this idea" [of man's quest to satisfy his spiritual hunger] into an intricate web of figures of speech and biblical allusions. She takes the idea of man's spiritual hunger literally and makes the parable of the loaves and fishes serve as a major—and thus controlling—image of the novel. What seems to be more obviously important images—fire and water—really derive from the loaves and fishes as she uses them, for loaves are baked, after all, and fish swim. . . . She teaches us to take her similes literally. . . . The dead . . . will receive the multiplied loaves and fishes if they are faithful. . . . 'Jesus is the bread of life,' the old man has told Tarwater, but the whole action of the novel consists in Tarwater's trying to escape this truth. . . . What he fears most and tries to run away from is what even he knows is the true object of his quest" (299-301) to satisfy his spiritual hunger. Trowbridge concludes that "at the end of the novel, when Tarwater accepts his role as prophet and starts toward the city, it is something within himself—the result of his acceptance of God's grace—that guides him, not any human figure. . . . Miss O'Connor seems to be emphasizing . . . the irresistible nature of God's grace" (305). This "something within himself . . . that guides him" is akin to that mysterious "something" within Norman Moonbloom in Wallant's *The Tenants of Moonbloom* (117) that motivates him into becoming a renewed human being.

Chapter 5

Methods of Presentation II
Symbols—Using People, Places, and Things

Edward Lewis Wallant and Flannery O'Connor, in their aim to compel us to see more than what appears to be, make extensive and significantly refined use of symbols in their fiction. Their characters, settings, and objects—natural and man-made—are all used to express the reality that informs the appearance of things. Just as Bishop's face in O'Connor's *The Violent Bear It Away* affects people with either awe or anger, so too does Norman Moonbloom's in Wallant's *The Tenants of Moonbloom*. Moonbloom's face is a cause of wonder and concern. Early in the novel, while immersed in himself, we read: "He walked lightly . . . his face showed no awareness of all . . . the thousands of people around him" (9). Still later: "For Norman the distance between him and the nearest passer-by was infinite" (49). Early in his life he feels he should reach out to others but doesn't. "He is alone and searching for a regret he cannot feel" (56). In this stage, he is like O'Connor's Raber in *The Violent Bear It Away*, who can feel "nothing" (241) after learning of Bishop's death. But Moonbloom, by his belated interaction with others, in his sharing their pain, is able to transform their pain and his own into joy. This transformation occurs when one is able to immerse himself in others, when one thinks of the other first.

It is Sugarman, the salesman, who first notices Norman's changing face. "You have a look . . . you come along . . . to what purpose? God knows. . . . If we are wrong, it is the fault of your face—it is a fraud. Change your face, Moonbloom, or else listen and do something for us" (94). Norman's face, like Bishop's, assumes symbolic religious overtones. It is a face that seems to prompt hope in the mind of the on-looker. Milly Leopold is another who notes Norman's face: "I'm sure you're not like the other agents. . . . I can see by your face" (89). Even the hate-filled Ilse Moeller "stares at him . . . fascinated by something just below his hairline" (90). When he decides to help the tenants rather than reject them, "his face seemed to sparkle as at the idea of a Holy war" (117). As the tenants begin to recognize his transformation—"He seemed eminently trustworthy as ideal for confidences as a religious image" (130)—his face takes on saintly connotations to others.

In Wallant's *The Children at the Gate*, it is Sammy's face that invokes spiritual connotations. His face deeply affects the patients at the Sacred Heart Hospital: His "skinny face bent enigmatically over a patient. . . ." (59). The "mysterious yearning on a patient's face appeared to be love" (60). After trying to sell people on the idea of forgiveness, he is beaten and badgered, yet is Christ-like in aspect. "His eyes [in his persecution] were tranquil under the mask of tragedy" (149). He sorrows not for all the beatings inflicted on his body but for all those inflicted on his soul because his pleas have fallen on hardened hearts.

The other characters in *The Children at the Gate* are also used symbolically. In this novel, Wallant addresses the seeds of corrosive evil we all have in ourselves. In the scene that takes place after the news circulates that a hospital orderly had attempted to molest young Maria Alvarez, a patient in the hospital, we read how Angelo, Nurse Sullivan, and others represent man's tendency to self-righteousness, in which we castigate the evil committed by others to relieve ourselves of guilt feelings over sins we have covertly committed in thought or in act. We absorb our potential for evil into the person of another. We believe that by judging others, we may somehow, to a degree, cleanse ourselves of that very same evil conduct that festers in ourselves. Wallant writes of the hospital staff who have just heard of the crime of Lebedov, the orderly: "No one dared to stand alone" (82). We all know any man is capable of the most degrading acts. Nurse Sullivan stands as a symbol of one who yields to self-righteous feelings that place her, she thinks, on a spiritual level above others: "'Someone tried to rape one of the kids in the pavilion,' she said in a low, quavering voice that had a certain angry pleasure in it" (87). What she does not seem to realize is that her attitude reduces her level of spirituality. Wallant, indeed knows human nature well.

In *The Pawnbroker*, Wallant's drawing of his minor characters is germane to his spiritual vision. This connection may be seen in his description of the "jawless man" (253), who stands as a symbol of fragile humanity in whom good and evil are components of man's earthly make-up. He is characterized by features both ugly and beautiful: "He had no jaw . . . but from behind, the sickened pawnbroker noticed how shapely his head was, how broad his shoulders above the tapering graceful torso" (253). And in what appears to be an innocuous, inconsequential afterthought, Wallant presents one of Nazerman's customers: "A smiling postman [who] pawned a dazzling pair of shoes, and whose smile was flat and shallow, because he appeared to live in a pocket of time only five minutes wide" (255). In contrast to his other memorable—at times grotesque—characters, the postman appears to symbolize empirical man, whose preoccupation is only with this material world, a subtle alter-ego for the pawnbroker himself, whose self-governing rule is to cauterize thought and live only in and for the present: "Life is here and now" (120). Nazerman's philosophy is given subtle concrete form in the person of this mindless "smiling postman" (225).

In Flannery O'Connor's *Wise Blood*, character is also used symbolically to augment her theme. In this novel, the force of evil is aggressive and tenacious in its attempts to capture men's souls. Young Sabbath Hawks, physically and spiritually ugly, proves a wily adversary of the good. She preys on Hazel Motes' pride, for Hazel defiantly disdains any outside help in fending off evil. "He had a strong confidence in his power to resist evil. . . . He trusted himself to get back [from military service] uncorrupted" (17), which does not happen. Sabbath knows man is vulnerable to temptation. "He couldn't leave off following me," she said. "Sometimes it is that way with them" (99). And a little later in her role as temptress: "He ain't used to me yet—but he'll get used to me" (100). Evil, O'Connor realizes, is subtle, persistent, and with many, a progressive disease. It is man's overweening pride, his self-indulgent ego, that makes him open to the chameleon faces and forces of evil.

Sabbath is one who knows Motes well. In her relationship with the "shrunken man" (51) who is the epitome of the completely lost soul, one imprisoned in the grip of death eternal, she stands as the agent of this doomed Devil figure. It is she who allies Motes to this lost creature. "She had been looking at Haze as if he were in a booth at the fair" (37). Earlier, we had read of "a man in a glass case, the shrunken man" (79). In reference to her relationship with the shrunken man, we read: "There was something in him of everyone she had ever known, as if they had all been rolled [into] one person and killed and shrunk and dried" (96). Just as Wallant implied in *The Children at the Gate*, O'Connor is reminding us that all men are susceptible to the forces of evil. Just before his conversion and just after her having had "relations:" with him, Sabbath asks Motes, "When are you going?: to which he replies, "After I get some sleep" (103). This exchange is followed by her astute realization that his now awakening conscience will not allow this rest. "You ain't going to get none" (103).

O'Connor is subtle in her symbolic references that denote characterization. She uses some seemingly insignificant people to lend insight into her protagonist, Hazel Motes. One who partakes of Motes' descent into evil is Asa Hawks, a preacher in despair. Ironically, in his hopeless state, he is able to see in Motes what Motes fails to see. As a sinner who has lost hope in being redeemed, Hawks knows the anguish of sin. He knows both sides of Motes: "I can smell the sin on your breath [and] I can hear the urge for Jesus in your voice" (31). He notes Motes' present condition and prophesizes his final destiny. "You got eyes [but] see not, ears [but] hear not. But you'll have to see sometime" (33). Hawks serves as a foil to Motes in that he is "a fake blind man" (64) who lacked the courage to truly see. He was unable to blind himself to this worldly existence as Motes later does. He rationalizes his failure by trying to convince himself that Jesus beckoned him to do it. As a result, he suffered guilt pangs, and thinking, "his face thoughtful and evil" (62), he finds pleasure in the thought that Motes too will be seduced into evil even though he senses Motes' final salvific fate. He is a man torn by his inability to practice what he had preached.

Solace Layfield, who appears as Motes' double, is immediately recognized by Motes as one who is the inverse of himself. Like Motes, he professes a disbelief in Christ, but Motes knows he does not mean it. As Layfield lies near death, he cries out for Jesus, but Motes, as false priest, "leans his head over to hear his confession" (111), and rather than offering this believer consolation and forgiveness, strikes him a fatal blow. At this point in the novel, Motes' denial of Christ is at its zenith.

When Thomas Lorch writes that "in Miss O'Connor's handling of the subordinate characters, particularly Enoch Emery, lies the major weakness of the novel . . . and it is difficult if not impossible to justify the extent of Enoch's role" (71), nothing could be further from the truth. In the novel, Enoch Emery stands as one of Motes' chief antagonists. He tells Motes, in his devilish pride, "You act like you got wiser blood than anyone else. I'm the one that has it. Not you" (36). But in the novel, this devilish creature fails to overcome the latent goodness in man's heart. O'Connor describes the gradual change in Emery as he wills his own spiritual decline. He hates animals because they act naturally. As a man bent on evil, he acts without thinking, like an animal: "He realized with a sudden intuition" (74) [that] he acts entirely on instinct. As he deteriorates, we read of his passing into the body of an animal: "The animals were a form he had to get through" (54) before he can achieve his goal—becoming in essence completely animal-like. He "was not very fond of children but children always seemed to like to look at him" (96). Children, it appears, seem to realize his oddity, his twisted nature that they sense as more animal than man. His adoration of "the shrunken man" (57), whom he places in an enclosure resembling a tabernacle, reveals his warped dedication to man at his lowest level, man without any sign of goodness within him. O'Connor summarizes his pitiful transformation from man to something lower than animals. "No gorilla . . . was happier . . . than the one, whose god had finally rewarded it" (102). People flee at the sight of this devil-in-disguise, a "creature hideous and black" (102), one whose exterior betrays his inner pernicious condition.

Place, as symbol, in both writers' work, may be viewed as evil. Speaking in particular of the city as place, Ted R. Spivey links O'Connor to James Joyce. Spivey says that "the great symbol of alienation for both Joyce and O'Connor was the megalopolitan modern city, that urban sprawl which had been cut loose from the moorings of earlier centers of cultural development that once formed the basis for those cities" (Spivey a92).

According to Leo Gurko, the city for Wallant "was the absolute nadir of the human line . . . a nightmare" (254). He notes that in *The Pawnbroker*, "it is in the urban hell that [Sol Nazerman] must be harrowed and find the terms of his redemption" (257), and in *The Children at the Gate*, Angelo "is . . . a pure urban type—smart, cynical, hardfaced, and little more than a boy, almost prematurely old" (258). Yet despite his estimation that Wallant's city "is a nightmare," Gurko also says that "it contains some inscrutable source within itself the seeds of its own regeneration. . . . Wallant believes uncannily in the regenerative powers of the city and his novels bear intimate witness to the rebirth of his wounded characters" (254). It seems valid to say that the "inscrutable source" and "the regenerative powers of the city" lie for Wallant in the hearts of the people, those affected by that mysterious "something" that Wallant repeats over and over again in *The Tenants of Moonbloom* (117).

In both writers' work, place also refer to an individual's "moral universe" (Cleary 34), a place where the character reflects his particular vision of the world. In Wallant's *The Tenants of Moonbloom*, it is the city's inhabitants who prove the catalyst to Norman Moonbloom's self-awakening. The despairing state of the city's environment awakens Norman to the fact that he is not alone in the world. He comes to realize that the forlorn-looking tenements hold within their walls people of value, desperately in need of being recognized as human beings. "Something" (117) emanates from the city's environs, from the heart of the city that resurrects Norman. His pains, real and imagined, no longer haunt him; they become paradoxically, sources of ineffable joy. The city's tenants open to him an avenue of spiritual and emotional growth, and because of them he is finally able to free himself from an environment that fostered, like a deadly virus, a death-in-life existence. We read: "Norman, staring out at the windy street with its scuddings of paper and bent-over people, appreciated the deep courtesy that could occur between people, a courtesy that many aristocratic in name, who would sooner die than belch in company, had no idea of" (137). The effect of the city and its inhabitants have transformed Norman into a new man.

In *The Pawnbroker*, Sol Nazerman seeks to escape to a more personal place, a place that threatens his humanity. Wallant describes Nazerman's pawnshop as looking like some "ancient remains half buried in the muck of the ocean bottom" (28) and like a "little cage" (41) and a "darkened vault" (224). The shop has a profoundly deleterious effect on the pawnbroker's vision, which was "darkened in expectation of the florescent dimness" (149). The shop, as place, is finally felt as a suffocating cell of isolation. "He bumped blindly in the narrow confines of the space behind the counter. He felt he moved at the bottom of some infinitely deep well and his hands groped for the dark sides. . . . He felt a terrific desire to get out of the store . . . the small insulated chamber he had dwelt in" (7).

The environment in *The Children at the Gate*, where Angelo works, is similar in character to Nazerman's pawnshop. "The store was overloaded with stock and there was a constant creaking, as though at any moment the whole place might collapse under its weight" (13). In both novels, "place," with its emphasis on material things, reflects the stress the characters confer on such things. Both Nazerman and Angelo preoccupy themselves with material things, not strictly for any desire to accumulate wealth, but rather as a means of evading any thoughts that deal with the meaning of existence. They attempt to "keep busy" to evade any inquiry into mystery, into the inexplicable happenings in life, into the reasons for men's sacrificial acts which, ironically, prove life-saving to them both.

Michael Cleary thinks that, in Flannery O'Connor, "the environment of the city affects its inhabitants in a negative way" (30). He argues that "the environment of the city or country can change the attitude and behavior of O'Connor's characters. [And their] altered behavior . . . [may be] partly attributed to the moral osmosis effected by the environment" (33). Cleary says that "the jaded city dwellers . . . like outcast demons . . . mock that which they cannot have." This attitude he sees is evident in *Wise Blood*. "Haze notes that its residents are oblivious to nature in any form, in part because of their obsession with commerce. Walking around Taulkinham, [he] remarks that 'No one was paying any attention to the sky'" (Cleary 30), referring in symbolic terms to the presence of God in the world.

In *The Violent Bear It Away*, Tarwater is caught up in the city, a place of peril, and to his credit he perceives its decadent state. He awakens to the knowledge that the city is a place in dire need of spiritual regeneration: "Intermittently the boy's [Tarwater] jagged shadow slanted across the road in front of him as if it cleared a rough path toward his goal. His singed eyes, black in their deep sockets, seemed already to envision the fate that awaited him but he moved steadily on, his face set toward the dark city, where the children of God lay sleeping: (118).

In O'Connor, then, the city may be viewed as a place ripe for a spiritual renewal. "O'Connor's quester seeks the values offered by the modern megalopolis, but [instead] finds at last . . . that he must prophesy to megalopolis, must cry out for a renewal of civilization's deepest values embodied for him in the image of Christ—in order for there to be a new city, a city of God" (Spivey a94). Spivey says, "O'Connor . . . speaks in [her] last works of a death of one cultural order that makes way for another. The sprawling city without order or direction is part of the necessary journey to this new order" (a95), this journey to the eternal city.

Many objects, animate and inanimate, and those elements necessary in sustaining men's lives, are used as symbols in both writers' fiction. One of the most prominent used by Wallant and O'Connor is the sound of silence or the absence of sound. In Wallant's world, both sounds and silence have beneficial effects. In *The Tenants of Moonbloom*, it is when

Norman "steps into the sound" (110) of humanity that he achieves full status as a member of the human race. Carol Hauser's "screams [over the death of her child, Bobby] made welts on Norman's insides" (110). "The high scream breaks...the lump of the hidden child enters Norman's stomach or heart or soul" (112); he can no longer immerse himself into the self. "Part of him knew that the gigantic city pulsed and moved in its intricate life oblivious to the one smothered cell and yet to him death had appeared for the very first time" (111). He is finally able to vanquish his fears and accept pain, sorrow, and death as the hard elemental realities of life. Until the sound of Carol Hauser's "high scream" (111) jolted him, "he had never considered that the state of being fully alive might be impending" (31). Other sounds also affect him in a way that awakens him to the brotherhood of men. As he moves out of himself, "the hollow coughing from a distant apartment, the child's ranting from another, alarmed him by their intimation of great size" (74).

In *The Human Season*, it is the sound of the river that demands one's attention. It is a sound that will not go away. It is the sound that becalms and sanctifies Joe Berman's soul. His later spiritual awakening has its roots in his childhood, when, overwhelmed by love for his father, he remembered it as a time of singing glory. "He thought he felt the presence of God in unique vestments and the world was filled with a peculiar singing mystery as he walked hand in hand with his father" (150). He remembers "the river singing" (141). He asks himself, "was it nothing when he heard the river deep and soft going on and on without stop, and heard his father speaking above the roar, his father and God in one tumultuous voice with the living water?" (159).

In *The Pawnbroker*, Nazerman sings a melody of death without first realizing it—it makes him choke. "Dy, dy, dy, dydidy, dy do . . . suddenly the sound caught him like a hook in his heart" (154). He is without any hope for the future at this time in his life, but at the end of the novel, his song of death of the spirit is heard no more.

In *The Children at the Gate*, Angelo finally listens to Sammy's injunction "to close his eyes and listen to the nothing" (161), We read: "He never wanted to miss hearing what happened in silence" (183). He has finally listened to Sammy's life-saving counsel though it took Sammy's supreme sacrifice for him to do it.

In Flannery O'Connor's *The Violent Bear It Away*, she emphasizes the sound of silence in Tarwater's journey to salvation. It is silence that conjures up the presence of God, a God ever-present in this world and in eternity: "It was as if [Tarwater] were alone in the presence of an immense silent eye. . . . The quiet seemed palpable, waiting. It seemed almost to be waiting patiently, biding its time until it should reveal itself and demand to be named" (174). The silence is ready to confront any form of evil. There is, O'Connor is telling us, a continual battle between man's choosing the good or submitting to evil. "It was a strange, waiting silence. . . . His mind had been engaged in a continual struggle with the silence that confronted him" (218). This conflict in Tarwater pits "silence" against evil, the "wise voice, the stranger" (137) within himself. O'Connor foreshadows the ultimate outcome: "The silence was about to surround him and he was going to be lost in it forever" (219).

In this novel, Bishop, as the symbol of Christ, is intimate with silence. "Somewhere below them out of the silence a bird sounded four crystal notes. The child Bishop stopped, his breath held" (232), and a little later, "The boy's eyes were drowned in silence" (237). With these two sentences O'Connor illustrates the Blessed Trinity, symbolized by the implacable silence, Bishop, and the bird who represent Father, Son, and Holy Spirit. At the end of the novel, Tarwater is finally able to envision the "mystery [that] resided in the deep-filled quiet that pervaded everything" (265). The road to salvation no longer "looked like strange and alien territory" (265) as it once did when he thought his former devilish voice within him was his "friend" (219).

In Wallant's *The Children at the Gate*, a bird is also used in a most significant way. As a symbol of the good, it helps to invoke Angelo's complete transformation: "As he looked up at the high whiteness, a bird darted out of a dark rectangle and flew upward in ascending spirals against the flame-blue sky. He shaded his eyes to follow its flight" (184). Then trying to discount the bird as nothing more than a bird, he says to himself, "Just another . . . pigeon [then] a distant cascading sound . . . the word "boychik" [Sammy's name for him, filters through his being, and he cannot escape] "the clarity of sunlight" (184) that focuses his attention on the true meaning of his encounter with Sammy. Thus again, in language as subtle as O'Connor's, we see invoked here, in the intimate connection of the "sunlight," Sammy's voiced "boychik," and the bird, a fitting description of Father, Son, and Holy Spirit.

The sun and the sky and the rain are also used symbolically in Wallant and O'Connor to reflect the presence of God and his gratuitous gift of grace that helps men see the truth behind appearances and to feel the cleansing power of redemption through the workings of grace in men's souls. In *The Pawnbroker*, we read of a "hot blue sky . . . all the bright light threatened him like a single massive flame, and he [Nazerman] was filled with a mysterious dread for the unusual emotion he now seemed to recognize—a sudden and unbearable loneliness. He saw himself as the last living creature on a burning orb . . . a gray figure . . . on the desolate landscape" (204-205). At this point, Nazerman's self-absorption, the cause of his despair, is at its peak.

In O'Connor's *The Violent Bear It Away*, the sun is used to signify O'Connor's feelings about the state of Tarwater's soul. When he is about to become enveloped in evil, we read: "The angry sun creeping behind the top-most fringe of trees" (150) appears ready to pounce on him. As he tries to escape the sun by drugging himself with alcohol, we read: "The sun red and mammoth was about to touch the treeline" (262). At this juncture, he is about to be enveloped by God, who aids him in his final positive rejection of the devil. Early in the novel, his mind is not filled with the spirit of God. The sky, like the sun, waits on him as he ponders his decision to fulfill his great uncle's prophesy, to preach the word of God. The sky at this point is a "white sky" (149), which he is "studying . . . through the leaves of the trees" (136). It continues to wait for his signature, for it is man's decision to write on the blank white, his final destiny.

In contrast to the sun's anger at Tarwater's initial fall, it beams in delight at Bishop. As Tarwater tries to dismiss his baptizing of Bishop as of small consequence, the sun will not cooperate: "The sun [was] like a large pearl, as if the sun and moon had fused a brilliant marriage. . . . Tarwater's narrowed eyes make a black spot on it. . . . He would have liked it to get out of the sky altogether" (255). The sun is all beneficence and all loving when it approaches its symbolic son, Bishop: "The sun which had been tacking from cloud to cloud emerged above a fountain [where Bishop is being baptized] and as a light [begins] falling more gently and rests like a hand on the child's white head" (221).

The rain, in both writers' works, is an even more obvious symbol, representing the cleansing, purifying power of God. When it rains, men are cleansed of their faults. It is a vitalizing blessing, given as a gift from the Creator. In *The Pawnbroker*, when Ortiz and his partners in crime make plans to rob Nazerman, the atmosphere is "starless and close [and] the air [is] filled with humidity . . . a choking blackness surrounds" (235) Ortiz. With deft, subtle irony, Wallant writes: "Each of them moved off through the light-torn darkness" (235). None wished to be revealed.

None wished to be cleansed. "Let's break up before it rains now" (235). But Wallant does not let Ortiz escape the stupendous moment of grace that finally overwhelms him. In a foreshadowing of his final renunciation of evil, we read: "The fiery exultation of evil drained out of him . . . he walked home, all hunched over, nailed heavily to the earth by the torrential downpour" (239). The rain, as a symbol of God's grace, will not allow Ortiz to escape. He was correct when he said, "The man on the cross weren't gonna do him no harm" (238).

In *The Children at the Gate*, the rain also serves as a reference to grace. In Angelo's case, it forces him to go outside of himself. He decides to confront mystery in the person of Sammy and the hospital, which symbolizes pain and suffering. As a symbol of grace, "The rain on his head relieved him and the building looked cozy with yellow light (125). Ironically, what he resists proves to be the byways to his conversion of heart—Sammy and the Sacred Heart Hospital. Both make him vulnerable to the workings of grace. When he says, "Let it rain' [to Sammy] he had a sensation of falling disastrously (133) into the irrational world of mystery and grace.

In O'Connor's *Wise Blood*, the rain prods Hazel Motes in his search for truth. "His eyes . . . don't look like they see what he's looking at but they keep on looking" (62). At this point, though he does not realize it, he is seeking something beyond the appearance of things, and just prior to his conversion, we read: "Drops of rain water were splattered . . . and they hung sparkling from the brim of his hat" (103). This symbolic rain appears an advent to Motes' spiritual change of heart.

And in reference to Motes' hat, we see another significant symbol that stands out conspicuously in *Wise Blood*. It first appears as he attempts to preach his own idea of a religion without Christ. When he is in the presence of Mrs. Watts, she removes his hat and mocks its religious connotations. When he is in the presence of evil, he is hatless, but at the end, just before his dramatic conversion, he wears a hat. It is at this point the policeman asks him, "Was you going anywheres?" (114). His negative reply symbolizes his realization that even with a hat, the apparent sign of a preacher, he still seems to be going nowhere; his church without Christ leads only to a dead end. Even the very color and texture of the hat are symbolic of Motes' gradual awakening to the presence of Christ. Early in the novel, it is "stiff" (144), and later, as he grows in his belief that he is his own savior, "the lines of the hat seemed to stiffen fiercely" (12), and still later, "His face stern and determined under the heavy hat" (14); it is as if his attempts to save himself prove much too burdensome. In the presence of evil—Mrs. Watts—the hat is "black" (31). When Motes decides to buy a car and seek self-isolation, "his black hat sat on his head with a careful placed expression" (34). At this point, his vying for worldly satisfactions is symbolized by the color and texture of the hat. Still later, after Mrs. Watts has destroyed his hat out of malice, signaling her repudiation of him because she knows he cannot bear to look at her when he is in a communal act of evil, he acquires a "new hat" (57) which "looked just as fierce as the other one had" (57). His "new hat" does nothing to improve his ability to distinguish between appearance and reality, between falsity and truth. When he discovers that Asa Hawks was not the good man he had thought him to be, "his expression seemed to open onto a deeper blankness . . . [and] he moved back expressionless under the white hat" (84). The "white hat" appears to emphasize his blank mind. In his pitiful self-immersion, he cannot think clearly. Still self-deceived, he becomes enraged when he sees his double, Solace Layfield, wearing a hat similar to his own. He feels he is being mocked, "Take off your hat, you ain't true. You believe in Jesus" (86). O'Connor then writes: "The man didn't look so much like Haze lying on the ground . . . without his hat on" (114). Here O'Connor subtly declares the truth, for Layfield did believe in Christ. Haze's hat then may be seen as a primary symbol of self-delusion. It is the object that signifies his belief only in himself. In the final scene, after his spiritual awakening, we note that the hat has become "wheat colored" (118); it now has a natural look; it is a natural object somehow imbued with life. No longer is Motes in a world of white "blankness" where truth remains invisible; he is now close to nature, to fields of wheat, signs of God's wondrous creation.

Similarly, in *The Violent Bear It Away*, a hat is of symbolic significance. On first coming to the city, Tarwater wears his hat, as noted, a sign of a preacher. Seeing him with the hat on, the people ignore his presence. Then upon losing his hat, he becomes one with the worldly-minded city people. "He didn't observe the passing people who observed him now" (140). The city people believe he is now attuned to their worldly agenda, those blind to the presence of their immortal souls: "The ducked heads, the muttered words, the hastening away" (138). As in *Wise Blood*, the color of the hat plays a significant role in *The Violent Bear It Away*. We note the color gray is used to describe Tarwater's hat when he has not yet decided decisively for good or for evil. His hat is neither black nor white: it is the "gray" period of time when we ponder and ultimately choose our own fate. Like his brethren Hazel Motes, he makes a final choice.

Mr. Wallant also uses color for symbolic purposes. In *The Pawnbroker*, he uses the phrase "rock-colored" (50) to describe the pawnbroker. The words appear to denote Nazerman's indifferent feelings about George Smith and other pawnshop customers. Nazerman suffers George Smith, as we have mentioned, not out of love but out of self-indulgence. He does not show his true, ugly feelings toward this pathetic colored man. He is like a rock in his feelings toward his fellow man before Ortiz resurrects his spirit by his sacrifice.

In *The Human Season*, Wallant's use of the color green is subtly fused and pointedly symbolic. After Joe Berman's fight with his Irish co-worker, he lies in "a green-painted room" (75) with his joy submerging his physical pain; now many years later, as he witnesses another fight between two strangers, the color green is mentioned once more. "Suddenly the wind stopped, a great emptiness filled the world with a greenish light . . . the sky held them all, Berman and the rest of the witnesses and the two fighters, [and] for all their little motions of life they seemed like creatures caught in the dark, greenish stillness of the air" (151). In this scene the "overpowering presence" (76) of God seems to lie in wait, waiting for Berman to acknowledge God's "irrefutable" (115) presence. This green light is fleeting; it "doesn't last long" (160). Berman's final acceptance of God's presence in his life, though sincere, is tinged with "desperation" (160). He clings with desperate hope to the reality of God.

Chapter 6

Methods of Presentation III
The Grotesque—Exaggeration and Violence

Their use of the grotesque is another significant element that links O'Connor and Wallant. Both make pronounced use of this device. Robert Drake notes that "O'Connor's use of the grotesque can be regarded as an instance of shock tactic resorted to when nothing else will do 'for those who have eyes to see and see not, ears to hear and hear not.' [For her] grotesquerie represents . . . an outward and visible sign of an inward and spiritual disgrace" (439b). But in J. Oates Smith's view, in "A Temple of the Holy Ghost," just the opposite appears true. Smith says that "the freak in all his freakishness is a temple of the Holy Ghost, like it or not. "This is the way he wanted me to be and I ain't disputing His way'" (548). In O'Connor, it is the seemingly "normal" man who judges with a practical, empirical view the ways of the world, complacent in his rational mind-set that what appears to be is its true essential essence; it he who is the true grotesque. Paul Levine says that "in O'Connor . . . the truly deformed are those crippled by bourgeois complacency, the complacency of the morally and materially comfortable [whereas] the presence of grace will always be a grotesque manifestation" (105).

Smith agrees with Levine's view: "It is just these . . . the unthinking grotesques [who have no true knowledge of] a vision of reality" (Smith 549). Smith also thinks that "O'Connor's fiction is . . . surrealistic, [that] the initiation of man in the presence of the Divine demands not only a surrealistic style but a surrealistic landscape, for man cannot step outside a familiar environment and into the world of Christ and the prophets into Divine reality" (554). He concludes by saying, "O'Connor yokes forever sacred and secular images by violence, [and] it is the artificial arrangement of these images, in themselves grotesque, that leads to the construction of a vision that is not grotesque but harshly and defiantly spiritual" (546).

Although Wallant is not "harshly and defiantly spiritual," he is in his vision, capable of using the grotesque to make man see the spiritual reality that informs the material. Sanford E. Marovitz has noted that "Wallant uses a variety of singular figures, often grotesque [in which the protagonist] is enlightened into a spiritual awakening, into the underlying truth of human kinship, sympathy, and love" (172). Robert W. Lewis says that in Wallant's *The Tenants of Moonbloom* "to be human is to be stupid and absurd, not rational. . . . In Norman's sharpening vision of life, his surroundings are often surreal; appropriately the characters are grotesques" (79-80). Lewis concludes that "Wallant's tortured heroes . . . cannot find God irrelevant, let alone dead. . . . They must suffer, be crucified, and reborn" (82). For Wallant, then, just as for O'Connor, the grotesques are the truly real people, those who see beyond the appearance of things; the "rational" for them means total blindness. Both O'Connor and Wallant, in their comparable vision, accept mystery and realize "there is no solution" (Smith 559) to it.

And the methods by which both writers effected the grotesque are very similar. Both resorted to exaggeration. J. J. Quinn notes that in trying "to make the reader see, [O'Connor's] vision magnifies or exaggerates . . . the manifestation of the grotesque to make [meaning] clear for a hostile audience" (524). O'Connor herself said, "'I have to distort . . . in order to represent . . . both the mystery and the fact.'" (McCullagh 43). This assertion coincides with Wallant's similar belief that "for the writer and subsequently for the reader, things must be magnified. [He says] 'Call reading then, a sort of magnifying lens, a pair of aesthetic spectacles'" (Zacharaslewicz 280). It should also be pointed out that both writers were skillful visual artists as well as literary artists. Jan Nordby Gretland argues that "O'Connor's early cartooning, an art form which relies heavily on caricature . . . feeds directly into the abstracted exaggerations of [her] grotesque art" (63). Wallant too had artistic talent, and after graduating from the Pratt Institute, he pursued a career as an artist. He was a graphic artist who, shortly before his death, was art director for McCann-Erikson, an art agency in New York. It may be seen, then, that both used their inborn artistic talent in their fiction to induce others to see what they, the artists, saw and believed. They felt it necessary to draw with large, startling figures and to exaggerate often through means often violent.

What has been said of O'Connor's fiction may be applied equally to Wallant's. "There is much ugliness in the stories [and] . . . also a glorious apprehension of the vulgar—Both of them, paradoxically, chosen vessels, but there is [also] beauty and life and health—and at the core of it all, finally order and peace" (Gretlund 40). For both writers "the role of prophet was not prediction or pre-vision, but rather an accurate present vision of reality" (60). Gretlund also notes they used "violence as a constructive force to reveal what is most essential in a character" (59). When one thinks of the acts of sacrifice committed by Jesus Ortiz in *The Pawnbroker* and by Sammy in *The Children at the Gate*, Wallant's vision of man's essential being is very much in sympathy with O'Connor's. Both knew man is more than body.

Chapter 7

Methods of Presentation IV
Imagery—Realistic and Romantic

The realistic imagery of their fiction is another facet that links O'Connor and Wallant. Raney Stanford thought Wallant was "able to use realism in a simple yet profound way" [Stanford 396). Stanford said, "It is his ability to mirror inner states through outer signs of seeming simplicity that is the secret of Wallant's realism" (395). This comment can easily be addressed to O'Connor's use of realism. Maurice Levy notes that "O'Connor's writing [illustrates] a Catholic writing with more than all the thematic structure built on sacristy, since it integrates the richness and weight of reality" (Levy 158). Stanford's further comment that "expanding minor mannerism into major revelation is the hallmark of an extraordinary talent" (Stanford 396) may be applied to both writers.

Their exacting use of words is a key element in their provocative realism. Speaking of O'Connor's "The Displaced Person," Arthur Kinney notes, "Like everything else O'Connor wrote, this is exactingly worded" (Kinney 89). And Whitney Balliet in his review of *The Pawnbroker* said that "Wallant [is] a rare combination—a first rate storyteller [and] a master of homely detail" (Balliet 210-213).

In addition to their realistic touch, both Wallant and O'Connor shared an affinity for the Romantic mode in their literature. Sanford E. Marovitz contends that Wallant is immersed "in the affairs of the New Romanticism with its moral concern, sincerity, mystical turns, and imperative call to action" (Marovitz 173). He thinks that *The Children at the Gate* "offers the clearest statement in his fiction of the Romantic [or mystical] theme" (Marovitz 177).

Virginia F. Wray notes O'Connor's explicit connection to "the world explored by Romantic writers . . . a world of two realms, the empirically knowable and the unknowable" (Wray 85). Wray cites O'Connor's "working aesthetic theory out of which her stories and novels grew, [as her] conception of nature . . . the aim of [which] is remarkably similar to that held by Nineteenth Century American Romantic [writers]" (85). Wray stresses that "the central aesthetic issue upon which O'Connor repeatedly focuses [is] the theoretical aim and practical means of metaphor to fuse the knowable and the directly unknowable realms of human experience into a single realm" (85). She is like Hawthorne before her who "sought for fiction a larger realm than just the empirically knowable particulars of time and place" (86) [and who said] he didn't write novels [but rather] Romances, [to which] O'Connor remarked, "I am one of his descendents" (89). O'Connor also agrees with Henry James, who said, "The source of a Romance is . . . an author's . . . feeling and seeing, of his conceiving . . . of one value or the other. [James believed} the Romantic signifies things that we can never know directly about" (Wray 90). In consonance with these ideas, O'Connor thought that "the novelist must be characterized not by his function but by his vision" (Wray 90). Wallant's vision, in its spiritual focus on man's regeneration and redemption by means of pain-filled joy, is at one with O'Connor's. His "mystical turns and call for action" (Marovitz 173) are reflected in all of O'Connor's fiction just as they are in his own. Romance for each was synonymous with mystery, essentially the mystery of man and the meaning of his existence. One final thread in the sphere of Romance that connects Wallant and O'Connor is the influence of Dostoyevski on them. For Wallant, "Dostoyevski is the writer whose novels moved him most . . . in him people were so complex, so intensely human . . . that I felt I had been living on another planet" (Ayo 87). Gerald R. Russello also sees Dostoyevski's influence . . . on O'Connor: "Although no friend to Roman Catholicism [Dostoyevski] altered the realism of Flaubert and Zola to allow the introduction of spiritual elements" (Russello 208) of which O'Connor made such profound use. Like Dostoyevski and Wallant, O'Connor looked beyond man's appearance into his very soul.

Chapter 8

Humor and Compassion

Humor and compassion are two signal elements that connect Wallant and O'Connor. In a Wallant novel, the ingredient of laughter is used as a soothing antidote to pain. In *The Tenants of Moonbloom*, Norman Moonbloom's acceptance of life, with all its inexplicable happenings, assuages his fear of pain. His former fear of pain is finally submerged and overcome by joy as a result of his thinking of others' pains rather than dwelling on his own.

Early in his life he is obsessed with fear of pain. "He sensed the imminence of pain" (63). "The thought of pain terrified him" (53), but during his transformation we read: "Norman, scarred, changing, looked into the depths for a beginning and caught a glimpse of it, heard the sound of it, a sort of awful yet uproarious laughter" (101) gripped him. He feels "an exquisite pain from his laughter . . . [and wonders] at his talent for laughing [and why] . . . had he chosen laughter. He could only guess at some instinct for survival, or some hereditary tendency to pray in a dance of joy" (118-120). For Norman, who is now "fully alive" (31) to others, laughter connotes a resurrection of the spirit; he no longer suffers a "melancholy contentment" (23). His joy is unbound, mocking even the pangs of pain. He is, as Sugarman said, "Hooked, addicted" (105) on life. At times "the old anticipation of pain came over him but it had no power to orient him now" (152). He now realizes "that joy resembled mourning, and was, if anything, just as powerful and profound" (117).

His joy is contagious; it affects the despairing Basellicci, whose cry, "I'm a dying man. . . . Let me alone" (154) does not dissuade Norman from persisting. As a result of his life-accented actions, he enables

"Basellicci [to] step outside his pain" (156). After they repair his toilet, "Basellicci began to laugh and cry at the same time. 'I'm drunk,' he wailed. 'I'm so drunk that I'm happy'" (156). Like Norman, he appears drunk with joy and happiness.

Laughter in Wallant is the result of a gradual awakening by the protagonist that despite its painful realities, life is still worth living. When one realizes this fact, he becomes alive with joy. Pain assumes a subordinate role. This is noted by David R. Mesher, who says: "Wallant's theme of redemption through suffering becomes redemption through humor in *The Tenants of Moonbloom*" (2931A).

In O'Connor, laughter is evoked not in the character, but in the reader. Her humorous jabs at man's egotism is a means to alert the reader to his self-possessed notion of reality, a reality that concerns itself only with man's earthly existence. In both writers' work, laughter is a way of seeing. In both fictions, the characters and the readers are called to see that "nothing is as it looks" (*The Childen at the Gate* 66).

Both O'Connor and Wallant have a dry, exquisite sense of humor. In O'Connor's *Wise Blood*, Enoch Emery remarks about Hazel Motes' lack of humor as he ponders Motes' social station in the world. His conclusion, though erroneous, makes its subtle, humorous point. "You don't ever laugh. I wouldn't be surprised if you wasn't a real wealthy man" (30). Mrs. Flood, Motes' landlady, is also needled in a light-hearted way by O'Connor when she voices her opinion on a person's normal behavior. She cannot fathom Motes' reason for blinding himself. "It's not normal. It's something people have quit doing—like . . . being a saint" (22). This comic scene reflects O'Connor's assessment of the modern, secular world's thinking. Her own personal belief that the church should maintain its quiet, dignified tone is seen in her assault on Evangelicalism: "The windshield wipers . . . made a great clatter like two idiots clapping in church" (38). O'Connor's barbs range far and wide.

In Wallant's *The Pawnbroker*, both light-hearted humor and deeply abrasive black humor are in evidence. Like O'Connor's Mrs. Flood, Jesus Ortiz's mother's naïveté is seen in the dispute she has with Mrs. Mapp, a Baptist. "It just happens Jesus Christ hisself was a Catholic [to which Mrs. Mapp replies] It happens he was a Jew. [Ortiz's mother replies in shock] Why, Mrs. Mapp, what a awful thing to say!" (87).

Wallant uses black humor, more biting than O'Connor's, to characterize Sol Nazerman's morbid attitude. In answer to Mendel's doctor who wonders how Mendel's body had "got like that [Mendel's body had been called a "crime"], Nazerman answers dryly, "A very bad accident of birth . . . He was in the camps" (191). This bitter remark underscores Nazerman's belief that life is one big joke. When the doctor informs Tessie that Mendel, her father, is dying, Nazerman's tart answer, "Who isn't, Doctor?" (192) reveals in its black humor the depth of his contempt for life.

In *The Children at the Gate*, as Louis Rubin has noted, Sammy's jokes have that distinct touch of "mocking irony" (Rubin 269) which he enjoys, but which grates on Angelo's sensitive nerves. In the scene where he parodies Jesus' miracle of "walking on the water" (*The Children at the Gate* 47), he expects to get Angelo to react in anger, and he does. "Angelo grimaced, 'I don't care what you were doing but don't ever try to pull the wool over my eyes'. . . . He smiled coldly" (47). "The fact was, he realized Sammy was teasing him. . . . The guy is a nut, that's all" (48). But Sammy's "jokes" give him no rest. "How can I let him drive me out of my mind? It's ridiculous" (164). "If there were no Sammy, he thought, he could stand up quite comfortably to all the rest of them" (140), meaning all those, who, unlike himself, preferred social contact rather than deliberate isolation.

Wallant, in his humor, like O'Connor, follows Henri Bergson's definition of humor, particularly when they employ black, biting humor. "Bergson suggests that comedy depends upon extreme objectivity. . . . Its appeal is to intelligence, pure and simple. . . . Indifference is its natural environment" (Martin 8). In Wallant's *The Pawnbroker*, Sol Nazerman certainly exhibits this type of humor as does O'Connor in characterizing Mrs. Flood's worldly attitude. Both Wallant and O'Connor use comedy for "socially significant or corrective reasons," [which Bergson maintains is one of its] "essential characteristics" (Currie 207).

Though both can sting in their pointed humor, neither O'Connor or Wallant lacks compassion. About O'Connor's compassion, Robert Drake notes that although "compassion is the quality O'Connor's fiction is supposed to lack, [she may be] a tough writer but she is not an inhumane one. . . . For Miss O'Connor, the wages of sin is still death; and she is powerless to intervene in the hellish consequences which overtake her prideful and self-justified villains" (218-219).

Bill Oliver adds, "She believed in another kind of compassion . . . [her] compassion . . . emerges most clearly from her handling of character" (3). Oliver continues, "Those characters who are suspicious of the world . . . miss most of its beauty and mystery. They do not have a sacramental view of life, which holds that grace comes to man, not in direct infusions from on high but through the things of this earth. It was the sacramental view that informed O'Connor's writings. . . . The endings of her stories do not merely punish her characters; they hint at the possibility of redemption for those who accept their initiation into suffering. . . . O'Connor's stories are so remarkable for their thunder and lightening and wind that the occasional gentle breeze passes almost unnoticed" (14).

William Koon thinks that O'Connor's compassionate side is illustrated in one way by her "gift of self-parody" (130). He says it is "the redeeming humility that is so important to [her] fiction that wields so much divine retribution. . . . Readers [he says] cannot fully appreciate the characters and their stories without recognizing the author's part of self-parody" (330). "Her prayer, 'Hep me not to be so mean' is real and dramatic. . . . It is the prayer of every believer old enough to recognize his doubts" (332).

Mark Boren reminds us that "in contrast to laughter that puts somebody down, [laughter in O'Connor] embraces the entire situation of humanity" (115), and Marion Montgomery argues that O'Connor's "position is . . . her recognition of the limits of art, not an indifference or hardness of heart" (102). Montgomery thinks "O'Connor brings us, along with her fictional characters, to a passage from hell to purgatory, but she respects both the freedom of her characters and her readers' wills and the mystery of God's providence too much to encourage judgment or . . . a suspension of judgment. . . . The reader who is left disturbed by her fiction . . . may find . . . his discomfit . . . to lie in his having been left with the problem of reconciling justice and mercy to sin. . . . As prophet, [Montgomery thinks], she recalls to us a known but forgotten truth that is disturbing, though we blame the story" (103).

J. M. G. LeClezio echoes Montgomery's sentiments when he says, "If a world that Flannery O'Connor created shocks us, it is not so much because it is confused and brutal, but because it is true. With its harsh, plain, intuitive and demanding truth, it is there to uproot our illusions, to convince us, to make us question what our senses and our minds tell us, and to make us love lucidity. . . . Such a book [as *The Violent Bear It Away*], in all of its despair and its cruelty, in its language that talks endlessly of persecution, hatred and death, can only be the work of someone who loves life passionately, loving it as it is, with both joy and pity . . . [for] the very essence of existence is [within men]. . . . Life requires violence . . . revolt is active. It involves progress. It is a victory over death" (170, 172). In other words, Ms. O'Connor is telling us that we cannot sit still; we must break out of our complacency and see as she does that the grotesque is not a matter of physical deformity but of a blackened soul. The soul in the depths of depression and despair is equivalent to the death of the man. And for those on the opposite side of their secular status-quo, where anything is permissible and where self-justification replaces guilt, these also openly invite death eternal. O'Connor, in trying to make us realize sin is real, reveals her true love of man. Her metaphorical "devil is the one who goes about piercing pretensions, not the devil who goes about seeking whom he may devour" (Hawkes 99). She vies for the life of man's soul, not his death. If we are not able to see that her aim is compassion, it is because we are blind to the truth that sin is real and an active renunciation of it is mandatory.

O'Connor's "kind of compassion," as Oliver suggested, emanates from "her handling of character" (3). This character delineation may be seen in *The Violent Bear It Away* and in "The River," in which two children, Bishop and Bevel, are drowned. In both instances, their deaths are salvific. Bishop, as a symbol of Christ, dies in order that Tarwater may be saved, for in drowning Bishop, Tarwater simultaneously baptizes him into eternal life and by doing so gives himself the opportunity to follow in Bishop's footsteps. His act allows him to consider the meaning of his own Baptism and to change radically from the path of sin and self-destruction he had been bent on pursuing.

In "The River," the cynical Mr. Paradise cannot fathom young Bevel's act of deliberately drowning himself. For him, physical death means the death of life, whereas for Bevel, it is the way to life eternal. O'Connor is telling us that those immersed completely in this present life only, will never understand that our body is a "Temple of the Holy Ghost" and for this reason, for her, our physical death is not the end, but rather a new beginning.

In Wallant's case, "A theme that is in all his novels [is that] all his characters [have] to confront the sufferings of other people" (Fein 70-71). Man cannot be indifferent to his fellow man. He must reach out to others as Norman Moonbloom does in *The Tenants of Moonbloom*. Moonbloom's isolation before his spiritual recovery, as well as Angelo's, Berman's, and Nazerman's, reveal Wallant's deep concern for man's spiritual well-being. This idea is dramatized in Nazerman's and Angelo's cases by having their recovery paid for at the cost of another's life.

Both Wallant and O'Connor tell us we must remember there are others who have pain equal to our own. In *The Tenants of* Moonbloom and in *The Violent Bear It Away*, Moonbloom acts and Tarwater realizes he must do the same for his fellow human beings as each novel ends. Both tell us by serving others, we serve and save ourselves.

Chapter 9

Humanism: Secular and Christian and the Intertwining Philosophical Attitudes

The particular characteristic that appears to differentiate secular and Christian humanism is that in the former there is "a rejection of all forms of the supernatural" (Fox 237A) whereas in the latter the supernatural, or more precisely, the presence of God in the world, is a given fact. In both Wallant and in Flannery O'Connor, the supernatural is always in evidence. Their fiction asserts their shared belief that man's regeneration and redemption are made possible only by man's acceptance of God's pervasive presence.

Robert W. Lewis states that Wallant's "tortured heroes . . . cannot find God irrelevant, let alone dead. . . . They must suffer, be crucified, and reborn" (72). The Christian humanist believes that "God is the ground of all being [and] is the ultimate reality [and that] the world could be entirely separated from him only by ceasing to be. [He also believes that God] is contained in the natural even while transcending it" (Eggenschwiler 17, 19). As shown in his fiction, especially in *The Human Season*, Wallant is a firm believer in God's presence in the natural while "transcending it."

In considering Joe Berman's attempt to defy God and Sol Nazerman's similar attempts and their ultimate acceptance that God is not dead, it seems Wallant's humanistic stance leans toward the Christian rather than the secular. Even in the secular humanism of Paul Elmer More, there was emphasized . . . a call for . . . the subjection of action to a kind of "inner light" (Davis 9). And when one considers Wallant's continuous reference to the "inner light" in *The Human Season*, it may be said that he conjoins a modified secular humanism and a strong Christian philosophical stance. William V. Davis called him a "synthesizer" (10). Perhaps that is the best description of his spiritual outlook. Whatever we term him, his focus was always on man's relation to his fellow man and his relation to God.

David Galloway has noted that "Wallant's vision of life is profoundly religious, but never narrowly doctrinaire" (59), an idea with which Sanford E. Marovitz concurs: "Despite clear religious affiliations in all four novels, the doctrines of neither Catholicism nor Judaism determine the attitudes and behavior of the major characters" (180). Neither Wallant nor O'Connor were formally sectarian in their writings, but both were "ultimately concerned with [such] . . . spiritual matters as the truths of the human heart" (Wray 88). And just as Wallant proclaimed "I am not primarily concerned with Jewry. . . . I try to shape the larger human denominator" (Letter 1), so too does Miss O'Connor. As Robert Drake has noted, "She hardly ever referred to herself as a 'Christian writer' [rather] she usually described herself as a writer with 'Christian convictions' or 'Christian concerns'" (438-439). And George Lensing thinks O'Connor "though a Catholic . . . never attempts to impose a sectarian religious message" (172). He then adds, "She acknowledges the frailty of human nature and the constant struggle of [man] to overcome the dominance of self. [For her] the world contains . . . the co-existence of imperfection and redemption . . . the cohabitation of good and evil" (173-175). When considering Wallant's novels, cannot the very same thing be said of his beliefs? The fact remains that whatever tradition Wallant seemed to follow, the idea of God was always on his mind. He is in this respect akin in spirituality to Miss O'Connor. As Louis D. Rubin has astutely noted in his essay on O'Connor and Wallant, "Both Southerners and Jews have similar values different from modern times" (281). Mr. Rubin meant secular, positive times—scientifically-attuned times rather than religious.

When Wallant writes in *The Human Season*, that Joe Berman's "heart sang with a mysterious exultation that had no basis in reason" (Lorch 91b), he is walking in O'Connor's footsteps, for she thought "it reasonable to believe even though those beliefs are beyond reason" (Hawkins 93, 96). Both O'Connor and Wallant "shared a congenital drive toward the directly knowable [and they] controlled that drive by an adamant commitment to revealing the essential mysteries of human existence through appeal to ordinary, knowable situations" (Wray 92). Both knew they "could not approach the infinite directly, but must penetrate the natural human world as it is" (Wray 93).

O'Connor and Wallant believed in mystery, that things were not always what they seemed. Lorch tells us that Wallant "retains a deep awe and wonder at the goodness and beauty of man, and at the joy inherent in human existence" (91b). It is Wallant's ingrained spirituality that made him realize man's essence was more than his earthly existence, and that he is intimately connected to the "ground of all finite being" (Eggenschwiler 19). Kenneth C. Russell notes that in *The Pawnbroker* the main character passes from a state of withdrawal and non-feeling to a confession of life's goodness and an openness to others . . . as though some force breaks through to free him from the isolation in which he had taken refuge" (58). This "force" may validly be seen as Wallant's name for the presence of God. Wallant's own question, "Are we not . . . insane children hastening toward our extinction because we have struggled to extinguish those vast, elemental urges which argue for perpetuity, which ultimately affirm life itself?" (Marovitz 176). This "elemental urge" or mysterious "force" may be equated with that mysterious "something" (*The Tenants of Moonbloom* 45), which urges Norman Moonbloom to look at himself more closely and to emerge from his self-induced shell. All these terms may be seen in O'Connor as the spirit of God within us, something called *grace*, a gratuitous gift offered to us as a shield against the Devil's wiles, something we dearly need.

In Flannery O'Connor's fiction there are "epiphanies" or "special moments" [in] "the character's experience [which are] pure and universal . . . [and] God Himself seems to live again" (Levy 158-159). And in Wallant's *The Human Season*, Joe Berman experiences such a "special moment" when he and his father are transfixed by the felt presence of God as they stare at the peasants in the river scene. And just as O'Connor's "writing . . . forces the reader to go beyond the absurd to encounter mystery" (Levy 147), so too does Wallant, when we think of Sammy's absurd stories and actions in *The Children at the Gate*. It is the mystery of Sammy's being that causes the rational Angelo continual anxiety and frustration. Wallant's Angel and O'Connor's Rayber belittle mystery in their science-motivated, positivist attitudes. Angelo is more fortunate, however, in that he is saved by the sacrifice of another. For Rayber there was no "free vital relation with the existence and potentialities of the other" (Merton 18).

Wallant's novels, like *The Pawnbroker*, "point beyond what they reveal. [They make us] ponder . . . the wider questions of man's fate" (Becker 98). In Wallant's world "there are saintly clowns and clownish saints [here one thinks of Moonbloom and Sammy] . . . and both figures wage a battle of the spirit in a world of curtailed expectations [but] toward a refurbished vision of man" (Galloway 64).

When Thomas Merton says that O'Connor's philosophical point of view is "existentialist in nature [because it] is associated with the return to a Biblical mode of thought, which is entirely concrete and personal [and which] calls for a change of heart . . . a call of repentance [and] . . . the surrender of the free person to God" (Merton 19, 20, 22), we are reminded of Wallant's *The Human Season* in which Joe Berman recants his former denunciation of God, and acknowledges what he always knew to be true: "'Go on Berman,' he said in a hoarseness that was almost a whisper. 'Who you fooling? You knew all the time; inside you musta known what was out there in the dark. For a long time you knew it wasn't a God with a beard just out to get you'" (*The Human Season* 159).

It may be seen, then, that O'Connor's "grace" and Wallant's mystical and enigmatic "something" [can] obliterate all "obstacles and limitations, whether of sin, of selfishness, of fear and even of death [and] when this unseen, spiritual force makes its presence felt, it shows its possessor has reached a state of perfect and total reconciliation . . . with one's true self, one's neighbor and with God" (Merton 22). Thinking of O'Connor's Hazel Motes and Marion Francis Tarwater and Wallant's Joe Berman, Norman Moonbloom, and though to a lesser degree, Sol Nazerman, this statement by Merton appears to be well-illustrated dramatically in O'Connor's and Wallant's novels.

Merton labels O'Connor's philosophy "existential theology" because it "challenges the sterility and the inner helplessness, the spurious optimism and the real despair which masks itself in the secular and positivist illusion" (23). And though Merton is speaking only about O'Connor, it seems accurate to say his thoughts could be addressed equally to Mr. Wallant's fiction. One need only think of *The Children at the Gate* and Angelo DeMarco's role in that novel to see the validity of this finding, for under Angelo's optimistic facade lies a very vulnerable and despairing human being. He knows in his heart Sammy's "bugging" him is caused by Sammy's spiritual insight, by the spirit of truth within him.

In our reflections on the remarkable similarities that are reflected in the writings of Flannery O'Connor and Edward Lewis Wallant, the questions posited by Gerald R. Russello seem pertinent and revelatory. Russello asks "whether the influence of Catholic writers extends beyond Catholic circles and whether that influence has caused an integration between the Catholic imagination and American cultural life" (213). He then elucidates further: "Can we trace elements of the 'Catholic' imagination through aspects of American intellectual life other than Catholics" [He then posits a possible solution to his question]. "Perhaps we should be scanning contemporary authors for traces of Catholicism?" (213). Perhaps an answer can be found when we consider Nicholas Ayo's finding a "rich comparison" (86) between O'Connor's and Wallant's fiction. Though they never met nor knew each other, they appear mirror images of each other in the realm of their imagination. We have seen in their fiction a singular focus on the spiritual state of universal humanity; it is not difficult, therefore, to call their works "Catholic" in the sense of the term's universality, nor perhaps even in the religious sense of the term. Perhaps it is best to answer this question by quoting Seymour Epstein: "Only truth has the curious faculty of transcending all backgrounds and taking on that marvelous flexibility which gives to each reader his own personal application of the truth involved" (10). In reviewing their works, the two appear one in spirit, in heart, and in truth. And although labeling their philosophies may be of small significance, Wallant's spiritual leanings appear to issue forth and focus on God, the Father, the omnipresent power immanent in the world, whereas Miss O'Connor proclaims in all her writings the incarnate image of God the Father—Jesus Christ, His Divine Son.

Works Cited

Ayo, Nicholas, 1970. "The Secular Heart: The Achievement of Edward Lewis Wallant." *Critique* XII:86-94.

Balliett, Whitney, September 19, 1964. "Lament." *New Yorker*, 210-213.

Baumbach, Jonathan, 1965. *The Landscape of Nightmare*. New York: New York University press, 1-15, 138-151.

Becker, Ernest, 1969. *Angel in Armor*. New York: George Braziller Publication Co., 73-100.

Berger, Alan L., 1985. *Crisis and Covenant: The Holocaust in American Jewish Fiction*. Albany, NY:State University of New York Press, 164-172.

Boren, Mark, 1988. "Flannery O'Connor, Laughter, and the Word Made Flesh." *Flannery O'Connor: A Study of the Short Fiction*. Edited by Suzanne Morrow Paulson. Boston: Twayne Publishers, 115-119.

Browning, Preston, Jr., 1969. "'Parker's Back': Flannery O'Connor's Iconography of Salvation by Profanity." *Studies in Short Fiction*, 525-535.

Burns, Shannon, 1978. "The Literary Theory of Flannery O'Connor." *Flannery O'Connor Bulletin* 7:101-113.

Cleary, Michael, 1979. "Environmental Influences in Flannery O'Connor's Fiction." *Flannery O'Connor Bulletin*, 8:20-34.

Curley, Dan, 1988. "Flannery O'Connor and Moral Relativism." *Flannery O'Connor: A Study of the Short Fiction*. Edited by Suzanne Morrow Paulson. Boston: Twayne Publishers, 159-161.

Currie, Sheldon, 1988. "Flannery O'Connor's Comic Imagery." *Flannery O'Connor: A Study of the Short Fiction*. Edited by Suzanne Morrow Paulson. Boston: Twayne Publishers, 207-209.

Davis, William V., May 1968. "A Synthesis in the Contemporary Jewish Novel: Edward Lewis Wallant." *Cresset*, 8-12.

Works Cited

Desmond, John F., Winter 1990. "Walker Percy, Flannery O'Connor and the Holocaust." *The Southern Quarterly*, 28 (2)35-42.

Drake, Robert, 1988. "Flannery O'Connor's Compassion." *Flannery O'Connor:A Study of the Short Fiction*. Edited by Suzanne Morrow Paulson, Boston:Twayne Publishers, 218-219.

———, Robert, 1969. "The Paradigm of Flannery O'Connor's True Country." *Studies in Short Fiction* 6:433-442,

Dula, Martha A., 1972. "Evidences of the Prelapsarian in Flannery O'Connor's *Wise Blood*." Xavier University Studies, Vol. 11,1-12.

Eggenschwiler, David, 1972. *The Christian Humanism of Flannery O'Connor*. Detroit, MI: Wayne State University Press, 13-32.

Epstein, Seymour, May 10, 1965. "Edward Wallant's Legacy." *Congress Bi-Weekly*, 8-10.

Fein, Richard J., May 1969. "Homage to Edward Lewis Wallant." *Mainstream* 15:70-75

Fox, William Henry, 1979. "Opposition to Secular Humanism in the Fiction of Flannery O'Connor and Walker Percy." Doctoral Dissertation, Atlanta, GA: Emory University, 236, 237A.

Gallagher, Janet M., 1990. "Telling Stories About God: Narrative Voice and Espistomology in the Hebrew Bible and in the Fiction of Flannery O'Connor, Graham Greene and Cynthia Ozick." Doctoral Dissertation. Bronx, NY: Fordham University, 1221A.

Galloway, David D., Spring-Summer 1965. "Clown and Saint: The Hero in Current American Fiction." *Critique*, 46-64.

———, 1979. *Edward Lewis Wallant*. Boston: G. K. Hall & Co., 18-151.

Gretlund, Jan Nordby, 1987. Realist of Distances: Flannery O'Connor Revisited. Aarhus, Denmark: Aarhus University Press, 46-54.

Gurko, Leo, October 1974. "Edward Lewis Wallant as Urban Novelist." *Twentieth Century Literature*, 252-261.

Hawkes, John, 1985. "Flannery O'Connor's Devil." *Critical essays on Flannery O'Connor*. Edited by Melvin J. Friedman and Beverly Lyon Clark. Boston: G. K. Hall & Co., 92-100.

Hawkins, Peter, Spring 1982. "Faith and Doubt First Class: The Letters of Flannery O'Connor." *Southern Humanities Review* 16:91-103.

Hicks, Granville, 1970. *Literary Horizons: A Quarter Century of American Fiction*. Foreword by Granville Hicks. New York: New York University Press, 135-149.

Works Cited

Hoyt, Charles Ava, 1970. "The Sudden Hunger: An Essay on the Novels of Edward Lewis Wallant," *Minor American Novelists*. Edited by Charles Ava Hoyt, Carbondale: Southern Illinois University Press, 118-137.

Karpowitz, Stephen, Spring 1977. "Conscience and Cannibals: An Essay on Two Exemplary Tales—*Soul of Wood* and *The Pawnbroker*." *The Psychoanalytic Review* 64:41-62.

Kazin, Alfred, 1962. Back Cover. *3 by Flannery O'Connor*, Berginfield, NJ: The New American Library, Inc.

Kessler, Edward, 1988. "Flannery O'Connor's Poetic Metaphors." *Flannery O'Connor: A Study of the Short Fiction*. Edited by Suzanne Morrow Paulson. Boston: Twayne Publishers, 209-213

Kinney, Arthur F., Spring 1986. "Flannery O'Connor and the Fiction of Grace." *The Massachusetts Review*, 71-96.

Klein, Marcus, 1973. "Further Notes on the Dereliction of Culture: Edward Lewis Wallant and Bruce J. Friedman." *Contemporary American-Jewish Literature—Critical Essays*. Edited by Irving Malin, Bloomington, IN: Indiana University Press, 229-247.

Koon, William, April 1979. "Hep Me Not To Be So Mean: Flannery O'Connor's Subjectivity." *The Southern Review* XV:322-332.

Kremer, Lillian S., 1987. "From Buchenwald to Harlem: The Holocaust Universe of *The Pawnbroker*." *Literature, The Arts and The Holocaust*. Edited by Sanford Pinksker and Jack Fishel. Greenwood, FL: The Penkevill Publication Co., 59-78.

LeClezio, J. M. G., 1988. "The Parents' Fear of Death in Modern Civilization." *Flannery O'Connor: A Study of the Short Fiction*. Edited by Suzanne Morrow Paulson. Boston: Twayne Publishers, 157-159.

Lensing, George, Summer 1966. "De Chardin's Ideas in Flannery O'Connor." *Renascence* XVIII:171-175.

Levine, Paul, 1970. "Flannery O'Connor: The Soul of the Grotesque." *Minor American Novelists*. Edited by Charles Ava Hoyt. Carbondale, IL: Southern Illinois University Press, 95-117.

Levy, Maurice, 1988. "Catholic Writing and the Universal Themes of Suffering." *Flannery O'Connor: A Study of the Short Fiction*, Edited by Suzanne Morrow Paulson. Boston: Twayne Publishers, 157-159.

Lewis, Robert W., Winter 1972. "The Hung-Up Heroes of Edward Lewis Wallant." *Renascence*, 70-84.

Lorch, Thomas, 1968. "Flannery O'Connor: Christian Allegorist." *Critique* X:69-80.

———, 1967. "The Novels of Edward Lewis Wallant." *Chicago Review* 19:78-91.
Lyons, Bonnie K., 1987. "Seeing and Suffering in *The Pawnbroker* and *Mr. Sammler's Planet*." *Yiddish* 6:114-121.
Marovitz, Sanford E., Fall, 1985. "A Prophet in the Labyrinth: The Urban Romanticism of Edward Lewis Wallant." *Modern Language Studies* 15:172-183.
Martin, Carter, 1975. "Comedy and Humor in Flannery O'Connor's Fiction." *Flannery O'Connor Bulletin* 4:1-12.
McCullagh, James C., 1973. "Symbolism and the Religious Aesthetic: Flannery O'Connor's *Wise Blood*." *Flannery O'Connor Bulletin* 2:43-58.
Merton, Thomas, October-November 1965. "The Other Side of Despair: Notes on Christian Existentialism." *Critic* 24:12-23.
Mesher, David R., 1978. "The Novels of Edward Lewis Wallant." Doctoral Dissertation. St. Louis, MO: Washington University, *DAI*, 2931-A.
Montgomery, Marion, 1978. "The Artist as 'A Very Doubtful Jacob': A Reflection on Hawthorne and O'Connor." *The Southern Quarterly* 16:95-103.
Muller, Gilbert H., Autumn, 1969. "*The Violent Bear It Away*: Flannery O'Connor's Moral and Dramatic Sense." *Renascence* 22:17-25.
O'Connor, Flannery, 1962. *3 by Flannery O'Connor*. Berginfield, NJ: The New American Library, Inc.
———, 1980. *The Complete Stories of Flannery O'Connor*. New York: Farrar, Straus and Giroux
Oliver, Bill, 1986. "Flannery O'Connor's Compassion." *Flannery O'Connor Bulletin* 15:1-15.
Parks, John G., 1986. "The Grace of Suffering: The Fiction of Edward Lewis Wallant." *Studies in American Jewish Literature* 5:111-118.
Quinn, J. J., Winter 1973. "A Reading of Flannery O'Connor." *Thought*, 520-531.
Quinn, Sister M. Bernetta, O.S.F., 1980. "Flannery O'Connor, A Realist of Distances." *Women Writers of the Short Story: A Collection of Critical Essays*. Edited by Heather McClave. Englewood Cliffs, NJ: Prentice-Hall, Inc. 136-144.
Rabasca, Iris Conchita, 1996. "The Prophetic Voice and Vision of Flannery O'Connor: The Influence of the Old Testament Prophetic

Literature on Her Fiction." Doctoral Dissertation. Stony Brook, NY: Stony Brook University Press. *DAI* 56, No. 10, 3963A.

Raper, Anne Browning, 1986. *Edward Lewis Wallant: A Critical Study.* Chapel Hill, NC: North Carolina University Press.

Ribalow, Harold U. "The Legacy of Edward Lewis Wallant." *Chicago Jewish Forum* (1964):325-327.

Rubin, Louis D., 1967. "The Experience of Difference: Southerners and Jews." *The Curious Death of the Novel.* Baton Rouge, LA: Louisiana State University Press, 262-281.

Russell, Kenneth C., Fall 1980. "The Devil's Contemplative and the Miracle Rabbi. Two Novels: Golding's *Spire* and Wallant's *The Human Season.*" *Studia Mystica* 3:52-64.

Russello, Gerald R., Spring 1999. "A Different Discipline: The American Catholic Novel." *Renascence* 3:205-215.

Schroth, Raymond A., 1966. "Prisoner of Time." *America,* CXV, 98.

Schulz, Max F., 1969. *Radical Sophistication: Studies in Contemporary Jewish-American Novelists.* Athens, Ohio: Ohio University Press.

Shear, Walter, 1968. "Flannery O'Connor . . . Characters and Characterization." *Renascence* 20:140-146.

Smith, J. Oates, 1966. "Ritual and Violence in Flannery O'Connor." *Thought* 41:540-560.

Spivey, Ted R. Fall 1987. "Flannery O'Connor, James Joyce, and the City." *Studies in the Literary Imagination,* 87-95.

———, 1986. *The Writer as Shaman.* Macon, GA: Mercer University Press, 86-90.

Stanford, Raney, Spring 1969. "The Novels of Edward Lewis Wallant." *The Colorado Quarterly* 71:393-405.

Trowbridge, Clinton W., Spring 1968. "The Symbolic Vision of Flannery O'Connor: Patterns of Imagery in *The Vilent Bear it Away.*" *The Sewanee Review* 76:298-318.

Wallant, Edward Lewis, Fall 1963. *Teacher's Notebook in English* 1. Yale University: The Courtney-Beinecke Library.

———, Collection of Personal Letters, Addressee Unknown, Courtney-Bienecke Library, Yale University, 1-4.

———, 1980. *The Children at the Gate.* New York: Harcourt, Brace, Jovanovich, Inc.

———, 1964. *The Human Season.* New York: Berkley Pub. Corp.

———, 1978. *The Pawnbroker.* New York: Harcourt Brace & Co.

———, 1963. *The Tenants of Moonbloom*. New York: Popular Library Inc.

Wray, Viginia F., 1977. "Flannery O'Connor in the American Romance Tradition." *Flannery O'Connor Bulletin* 6:83-98.

Zacharasiewicz, Waldemar, 1995. *Images of Central Europe in Travelogues and Fiction by North American Writers*. Tubinguen, Germany: 268-282.

Index

allegory
  Children at the Gate, The
    (Wallant), 38
  Pawnbroker, The (Wallant), 29-30
  Wise Blood (O'Connor), 37
Allegory of Love, The (Lewis), 29
"Alvarez, Maria", 48
Ayo, Nicholas
  on O'Connor and Wallant, 9
  religious symbolism, Wallant's use
    of, 42

Balliet, Whitney, 65
"Basellecci", 67-68
Baumbach, Jonathan, 6
Becker, Ernest
  being, mystery of, 7
  Wallant, importance of, 2
being, mystery of, 2
  Children at the Gate, The
    (Wallant), 7, 13, 39
  Human Season, The (Wallant), 7,
    9-10
  Pawnbroker, The (Wallant), 7, 9
  Tenants of Moonbloom, The
    (Wallant), 7, 10-11, 45
  as theme, 5-14
  Violent Bear It Away, The
    (O'Connor), 13-14
Berger, Alan L.
  Holocaust, 17
  Pawnbroker, The (Wallant), 17

Bergson, 69
"Berman, Joe"
  being, mystery of, 7, 9-10
  enlightenment, 15, 58-59, 75
  isolation, 69
"Bevel, 71
"Birchfield, Marilyn, 26
"Bishop", 13, 55
  an allegorical figure, 40
  being, mystery of, 13-14
  as symbolic figure, 47, 55-56
Blake, William, 3
Boren, Mark, 70
Browning, Preston, Jr., 43-44
Bunyan, John, 37
Burns, Shannon, 3-4

"Chestny, Julian", 14
Children at the Gate, The (Wallant)
  animals as symbols, 55
  being, mystery of, 7, 12-13
  enlightenment, 75
  evil, problem of, 50-51
  humor, 69
  nature as symbol, 55-56
  New Romanticism, 65
  parables, use of, 39, 41-42
  place as symbol, 51-52
  redemption, quest for, 6
  religious symbolism in, 54
  sound as symbol, 53-54
  symbolism in, 51

vision, 3
"Circle in the Fire, The" (O'Connor)
   Holocaust, 19-20
   pride, 19-20
Cleary, Michael, 53
conscience
   Children at the Gate, The (Wallant), 12
   Pawnbroker, The (Wallant), 36
"Cope, Mrs."
   Holocaust, 19-20
   pride, 19-20

Davis, William V.
   Tenants of Moonbloom, The (Wallant), 41
   Wallant, humanism of, 73-74
   Wallant, religious universality of, 41
"DeMarco, Angelo"
   being, mystery of, 6, 13, 15, 39-40, 51
   conscience, 12
   enlightenment, 15, 52, 75-76
   evil, problem of, 48
   grace, 55, 57
   humor, 69
   isolation, 52, 69
   reason, 39
   redemption, quest for, 6, 40-41
   vision, 5
desire, 38
Desmond, John F., 19
"Displaced Person, The" (O'Connor), 20
   Holocaust, 20-21
   language, choice of, 65
Dostoyevski, Fyodor
   being, mystery of, 7
   influence of, 66
Drake, Robert
   compassion of O'Connor, 69
   grotesque, O'Connor's use of, 61

O'Connor, humanism of, 73
Dula, Martha, 5

Edward Lewis Wallant (Galloway), 21
"Emery, Enoch", 50
enlightenment
   Children at the Gate, The (Wallant), 15
   "Everything That Rises Must Converge" (O'Connor), 15
   Human Season, The (Wallant), 15
   Pawnbroker, The (Wallant), 15
   Tenants of Moonbloom, The (Wallant), 15
   Violent Bear It Away, The (O'Connor), 15
Epstein, Seymour, 1-2, 21, 77
"Everything That Rises Must Converge" (O'Connor), 14
evil, problem of
   Children at the Gate, The (Wallant), 50
   Wise Blood (O'Connor), 14

faith, 39-40
Fein, Richard, 15
Flannery O'Connor Bulletin, 10
"Flood, Mrs.", 14
   Grace, 14
   humor, 68-69
   redemption, quest for, 6-7
   vision, 1-3
Fox, 73

Gallagher, Janet M., 43
Galloway, David D.
   Edward Lewis Wallant, 21
   Holocaust, 21, 24-25
   Pawnbroker, The (Wallant), 21
   Wallant, humanism of, 73
   Wallant, importance of, 21
   Wallant, religious vision of, 1

Index

"Goberman", 23, 25, 30, 33, 37
Gordon, Sarah, x
grace
  "Everything That Rises Must Converge" (O'Connor), 14
  Violent Bear it Away, The (O'Connor), 13-14
  Wise Blood (O'Connor), 14
Gretlund, Jan Nordby
  grotesque, O'Connor's use of, 61
  violence, use of, 63
grotesque, use of, 61-61
  by O'Connor, 61-62
  Tenants of Moonbloom, The (Wallant), 62
"Guizac, Mr.", 21
Gurko, Leo, 51

"Harmon, Mrs., 24
"Hauser, Carol", 54
"Hawks, Asa", 58
"Hawks, Sabbath", 49
"Hetty", 126
Hicks, Granville
  O'Connor, importance of, x
  universality, religious, 3
Holocaust
  "Circle in the Fire, The" (O'Connor), 19-20
  "Displaced Person, The" (O'Connor), 20-21
  O'Connor, Flannery, 19
  Pawnbroker, The (Wallant), 18-19, 21-23
  "Revelation" (O'Connor), 20
  Wallant, Edward Lewis, 17-19
Hoyt, Charles Ava, xi
Human Season, The (Wallant)
  being, mystery of, 8-9, 43
  color as symbol, 59
  enlightenment, 15, 73-74
  humanism, 73-74
  insight, 2-3

sound as symbol, 54
humor
  Children at the Gate, The (Wallant), 69
  Pawnbroker, The (Wallant), 68-69
  Tenants of Moonbloom, The (Wallant), 67-68
  Wise Blood (O'Connor), 68-69

isolation
  Children at the Gate, The (Wallant), 51, 69
  Human Season, The (Wallant), 67
  Pawnbroker, The (Wallant), 35-36, 68

James, Henry, 66

"Kahan, Sammy Abel"
  as allegorical figure, 38-39, 41-42
  as alter-ego, 38
  being, mystery of, 7, 12, 54-55
  enlightenment, 75
  faith, 38-39
  humor, 69
  sacrifice, 6, 62, 69
  as symbolic figure, 48
Karpowitz, Stephen, 7
Kazin, Alfred, xi, 3
Kinney, Arthur, 65
Klein, Marcus, 41-42
Koon, William, 70
Kremer, Lillian S.
  Holocaust, 22
  redemption, quest for, 22-23

"Layfield, Solace", 50, 58
LeClezio, J. M. G.
  Compassion of O'Connor, 71
  Violent Bear It Away, The (O'Connor), 70
Lensing, George, 74
"Leopold, Milly", 48

Levine, Paul, 61
Levy, Maurice, 65
Lewis, C. S., 29
Lewis, Robert W.
  grotesque, Wallant's use of, 62
  Tenants of Moonbloom, The (Wallant), 62
  Wallant, humanism of, 73
Lorch, Thomas M.
  Children at the Gate, The (Wallant), 38
  Pawnbroker, The (Wallant), 29-30
  Wise Blood (O'Connor), 37, 50
Lyons, Bonnie, 22

"Mapp, Mrs.", 68
Marovitz, Sanford E.
  grotesque, Wallant's use of, 62
  Romanticism of Wallant, 66
  Wallant, humanism of, 75
  Wallant, religious universality of, 41
"McKenna", 38
"Mendel", 68
"Mendel, Tessie", 24, 35
Merton, Thomas, 76
"Miller, Howard", 40
Minor American Novelists (Hoyt, ed.), xi
"Moeller, Ilse", 48
Montgomery, Marion, 70
"Moonbloom, Norman"
  as allegorical figure, 42
  being, mystery of, 7, 10-11, 41, 45
  enlightenment, 15, 51-52, 54, 67-68
  feat, 55
  redemption, quest for, 6, 45
  as symbolic figure, 47
More, Paul Elmer, 73
"Motes, Hazel"
  evil, problem of, 49

grace, 15
humor, 68
pride, 49
redemption, quest for, 5-6, 37, 57-58
suffering, need for, 15
vision, 5, 50
"Murillo", 23, 30-31, 34

"Nazerman, Sol"
  as alter-ego, 35-37
  being, mystery of, 9-10, 35
  conscience, 36
  dreams, 24-28
  enlightenment, 15
  Holocaust, 17-18, 24-25
  humor, 69
  isolation, 34, 36, 49, 52, 59, 69
  redemption, quest for, 6, 23-24, 32, 37
  repentance, 23
  suffering, need for, 15

O'Connor, Flannery
  allegory, use of, 37, 41
  being, mystery of, 5-6, 75
  biblical allusions, use of, 42-44
  Catholicism of, 3
  "Circle in the Fire, The", 19-20
  compassion, 69-70
  "Displaced Person, The", 20-21, 65
  essence beyond existence, 2
  "Everything That Rises Must Converge", 15
  grace, 15, 45, 75-76
  grotesque, use of, 61-62
  Holocaust, 19-21
  humanism of, 72-75
  humor, use of, 67
  language, choice of, 65
  "Parker's Back", 44
  redemption, quest for, 5

religious universality of, 2-3
religious vision of, 74
"Revelation", 20
"River, The", 71
"Romanticism of, 65-66
suffering, 19
symbolism, use of, 47, 49-51, 53-56
violence, use of, 63
Violent Bear It Away, The, 13-15, 44-45, 53-56, 58, 70-72, 76
vision as metaphor, 2-4, 15, 37, 49-50, 53, 55, 65-66
Wise Blood, 5-6, 14, 37, 49-51, 53, 57-58, 68-69
Oliver, Bill, 69-70
"Ortiz Jesus"
   as allegorical figure, 30-31, 39
   as alter-ego, 35-37
   being, mystery of, 9-10, 30
   conscience, 36
   grace, 34
   isolation, 36-37
   sacrifice, 10, 15, 17-19, 21-25, 27-28, 31-33, 37, 63, 70
"Ortiz, Mrs.", 68

parables, use of, 40
"Paradise, Mr.", 71
"Parker's Back" (O'Connor), 43-44
Parks, John G., 7
Pawnbroker, The (Wallant)
   allegory, 29-30
   being, mystery of, 7, 9-10, 22, 75
   color as symbol, 59
   enlightenment, 15
   evil, problem of, 30, 49
   Holocaust, 17-19, 21-28
   humor, 68-69
   nature as symbol, 55-56
   place as symbol, 51-52
   redemption, quest for, 6, 18-19, 32

repentance, 23
sound as symbol, 54
structure, 24-27
suffering, need for, 17
"Paxton", 11
Pilgrim's Progress (Bunyan), 37
place, 57
pride
   "Circle in the Fire, The" (O'Connor), 19-20
   Wise Blood (O'Connor), 18

Quinn, J. J., 62
Quinn, Sister N. Bernetta, 43

Rabasca, Iris Conchita, 6
"Rayber", 13
reason, 13
rebirth, spiritual
   Children at the Gate, The (Wallant), 38
   as common theme, 2
   Wallant, Edward Lewis, 2
redemption, quest for
   Pawnbroker, The (Wallant), 6, 24, 34
   Tenants of Moonbloom, The (Wallant), 6
   Wise Blood (O'Connor), 6-7
repentance, 26
"Revelation" (O'Connor), 20
Ribalow, Harold U., 28
   Pawnbroker, The (Wallant), 27
   on Wallant, 28
"River, The" (O'Connor), 71
"Robinson", 33-35
Romanticism
   O'Connor, Flannery, 65-66
   Wallant, Edward Lewis, 65-66
Rubin, Louis D., 7
   Being, mystery of, 9
   Children at the Gate, The (Wallant), 7, 13, 39

on O'Connor and Wallant, 2
Russell, Kenneth C.
  Human Season, The (Wallant), 2
  Pawnbroker, The (Wallant), 75
Russello, Gerald, 3, 77

sacrifice, 6, 62, 69
  Children at the Gate, The (Wallant), 6, 63
  Pawnbroker, The (Wallant), 6, 10, 63
  redemption, quest for, 5-6, 10, 70
Schroth, Raymond, 18-19
Schulz, Max F., 15
self-dominance of, 2
Shear, Walter 2
"Shortley, Mr.", 21
"Shortley, Mrs.", 20-21
"Smith, George", 31, 34-35
Smith, J. Oates, 61
  grotesque, O'Connor's use of, 61-62
  violence, O'Connor's use of, 61-62
spirituality, 1-2
Spivy, Ted R.
  symbolism, O'Connor's use of, 51, 53
  universality, religious, 3
Stanford, Raney, 65
stress, reaction to, 5
suffering, need for
  Pawnbroker, The (Wallant), 17
  Violent Bear It Away, The (O'Connor), 17
  Wise Blood (O'Connor), 17
"Sugarman", 47
"Sullivan, Nurse", 48
"Sydney", 126
symbolism, use of
  Children at the Gate, The (Wallant), 47, 50-52, 54, 57

Human Season, The (Wallant), 47, 54
Pawnbroker, The (Wallant), 10, 49, 51-52, 54, 56-57, 59
Tenants of Moonbloom, The (Wallant), 47, 52
Violent Bear It Away, The (O'Connor), 47, 53-56, 58
Wise Blood (O'Connor), 5, 49-51, 57

"Tangee", 35
"Tarwater, Marion Francis"
  as allegorical figure, 44-45
  being, mystery of, 15
  enlightenment, 15, 53, 71
  redemption, quest for, 44-45, 53-54, 56, 58
  suffering, need for, 15
Tenants of Moonbloom, The (Wallant)
  being, mystery, 6, 10-11, 45
  compassion, 42
  enlightenment, 15
  humor, 67-68
  place as symbol, 51-52
  redemption, quest for, 6, 45, 72
  religious symbolism in, 41
  sound as symbol, 53-54
themes
  being, mystery of, 7, 13
  evil, problem of, 30-31, 33, 37, 40
  redemption, quest for, 40-41, 66
  sacrifice, 52
  suffering, need for, 5-6, 13, 62, 71
Trowbridge, Clinton, 44-45
"Turpin, Ruby"
  Holocaust, 19-20
  pride, 20

universality, religious, 2-3, 41

Violent Bear It Away, The
  (O'Connor)
  animals as symbols, 54-55
  being, mystery of, 13-14
  biblical allusions in, 42-44
  compassion, 70-71
  enlightenment, 15
  nature as symbol, 56
  objects as symbols, 58
  place as symbol, 53
  redemption, quest for, 44-45
  religious symbolism in, 55
  silence as symbol, 54-55
  suffering, need for, 13-14
vision
  Children at the Gate, The
    (Wallant), 6
  Pawnbroker, The (Wallant), 34-36
  Wise Blood (O'Connor), 6, 37

Wallant, Edward Lewis
  being, mystery of, 9, 15, 43, 74-75
  Children at the Gate, The, 6, 10-11, 14-15, 41-42, 45, 47, 51-54, 62, 67-68, 71-72, 75
  compassion, 69
  essence beyond existence, 2
  evil, problem of, 50
  grotesque, use of, 64
  Human Season, The, 2, 7-10, 15, 43, 54, 59, 73-76
  humanism of, 73-76
  language, choice of, 65
  Pawnbroker, The, 6-7, 9-10, 15, 17-19, 21-37, 49, 51-52, 54, 56-57, 59, 65, 68-69, 75-76
  religious symbolism, use of, 41-42
  religious universality of, 2-3, 41
  religious vision of, 2
  Romanticism of, 65
  seeing as metaphor, 2
  self, dominance of the, 1
  suffering, 21, 62, 69
  symbolism, use of, 47-49, 51-57, 59
  Tenants of Moonbloom, The, 7, 10-11, 14-15, 45, 47-48, 52-54, 67-68, 71-72
  violence, use of, 63
"Watts, Mrs.", 37, 57
"Wheatly, Mabel, 23, 34-35
Wise Blood (O'Connor)
  as allegorical novel, 37
  evil, problem of, 49-51
  humor, 68-69
  nature as symbol, 57
  objects as symbols, 57-58
  place as symbol, 53
  pride, 19
  redemption, quest for, 5, 37
  suffering, need for, 17
  vision, 5, 37
Wray, Virginia F., 66

Zacharasiewicz, Waldemar, 62

About the Author

Dr. McDermott received his bachelor's, master's and doctoral degrees from Fordham Universty, New York University, and St. John's University respectively. He is an adjunct professor of English at Farmingdale State University and at Suffolk Community College in New York. His published articles reveal his eclectic literary interests. William Faulkner, Flannery O'Connor, Wallace Stevens, D.H. Lawrence, Nathaniel Hawthorne, Albert Camus, Eugene Ionesco and William Shakespeare are some of the authors that have caught his interest. A lifelong New Yorker, he is married and has four children and resides in Lake Grove, N.Y.

www.ingramcontent.com/pod-product-compliance
Lightning Source LLC
Chambersburg PA
CBHW021133300426
44113CB00006B/406